# SHARING THE SANDBOX

Building and leading world-class teams in the 21st century.

**By Dean M. Brenner**
President
The Latimer Group

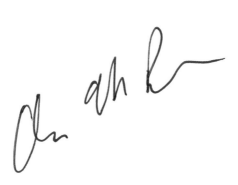

THE LATIMER GROUP

Dean M. Brenner – President
The Latimer Group
350 Center Place
Suite 203
Wallingford, CT 06492
Phone: 203.265.4344
www.thelatimergroup.com

ISBN # 978-0-9854357-0-7

First Edition

Printed in the United States of America.
10   9   8   7   6   5   4   3   2   1

## Dedication

*To my father, who made The Latimer Group and this book possible. Dad, your support of my sailing in the early years changed the course of my life, and the skills I leverage every day in my professional life come directly from you. I rarely said thank you while you were alive. So I say it now. Thank you, Dad.*

*And to my wife, Emily, and son, Zachary, who bring light to my heart and joy to my soul every single day. The two of you make life worth living.*

# Contents

# Acknowledgments

I've tried to draw on the experiences of my full life in the writing of this book, and along the way, I've been blessed to have had the opportunity to work with, and for, many great people. Additionally, I've had the opportunity to compete with and against some world-class athletes. While I can't mention all who have had an impact on my experiences, a few merit special mention:

- **The Latimer Group Board of Advisors.** Tom Lips, Mike Davis, Josh Levine, Bryan Gildenberg, Phil Bonanno, and Bill Goggins are the current board, and Bill McKendree, Elizabeth Riley, Jonathan Kelly, and Fred Whittemore have served in the past. All have provided outstanding advice and counsel at every stage of The Latimer Group's growth, helping us grow from the idea on the home office white board to a consultancy with global reach and clients on five continents.

- **The Olympic Sailing Committee Board.** Josh Adams, Bob Billingham, Louise Gleason, Carol Cronin, Zack Leonard, Ben Richardson, Jerelyn Biehl, Serge Jorgensen, Jim Tichenor, and Tim Wadlow have all served our Olympic Sailing Program faithfully and expertly the entire time I've served as chairman. You have set me straight on countless issues and provided sage advice and counsel on how to run a program time and time again.

- **My teammates on the British American Cup Sailing Team.** There are many of you, but you all know who you are. This group has had a significant impact on my life – you not only showed me how to win races, you showed me what the meaning of teamwork really is.

- **The athletes on the US Sailing Team.** The opportunity to serve you for the last eight years has been one of the great experiences and honors of my life. We've worked together, grown together, agreed and disagreed on many things, but always shared the common goal of representing the United States of America in the best way possible. Thank you.

- **Tom Lips.** Tom, you have been more than just a key member of our Board of Advisors. You have continuously looked for opportunities for The Latimer Group, and many of our key client relationships can be traced back to introductions from you. Thank you.

- **Kevin Cushing.** Kevin, you were not only the CEO of the title partner of the US Sailing Team, you are also a great friend and inspiration. I look forward to many more years of friendship and partnership. Thank you.

- **Gary Jobson.** Friend, mentor, colleague. Thanks for great guidance on countless issues, Gary, and for your steadfast support of the US Olympic and Paralympic Sailing Program.

- **Charlie Leighton.** Thanks for showing everyone around you how to manage and lead with a head and a heart. You are one of a kind, sir.

- **Ron Rosenberg.** You were my first real sailing coach, and you have remained a dear friend and voice of reason for the last 15 years.

- **Ed Baird, Tom Burnham, Tony Rey, and Reid McLaughlin.** I send a hearty thank you to my Soling teammates for our six-year effort to qualify for the 2000 US Olympic Sailing Team. This was one of the great team experiences of my life for all sorts of reasons. Thanks for teaching me how to race and for being part of a great blank canvas that allowed all of us to learn so much about ourselves.

- **The partners of The Latimer Group: Brett Slater at Slater's Garage, Mary Ann and Kyle Dostaler at MAD Communications, Laura Tedeschi at T2 Creative, and John Cunneen at AlphaGraphics New Haven.** Each of you has contributed substantively to this project and to so much that The Latimer Group creates. Thank you.

- **Phil Davis and the team at AG Books.** Your partnership and support of this project have been outstanding from start to finish. Thank you.

- **Pat Dennehy and Mike Velez.** The two of you have given me a front-row seat to your great work for the last seven years. You are great friends and world-class coaches, and it is joy to watch you work.

- **Dick Holliday, Bob Audette, and Bruce Avery.** I'll never forget the lessons of my mentors from my first days as an eager, aggressive but only modestly talented sailor in Watch Hill, Rhode Island. The three of you, each in your own way, have had a profound impact on my life as a sailor and a teammate.

- **Whitney Wall.** Thank you for keeping everything in line at The Latimer Group and for putting up with me every day. Bringing you onboard was one of the best business decisions I've ever made.

- **Sarah Adams.** You are a world-class editor, Sarah, with an uncanny ability to make my writing better without changing the "voice." Thank you.

- **My colleagues at US Sailing, past and present.** Gary Bodie, Kenneth Andreasen, Jack Gierhart, Dan Cooney, Dana Paxton, Dave Johnson, Katie Smith, Will Ricketson, and Katie Kelly. Each of you, in your own unique way, has taught me a great deal about how teams should work and what it takes to be a great teammate.

- **My entire family: Emily, Zach, Linda, Tony, Tom, Margah, Glen, Keri, and Evan.** Thanks for supporting me on this project and in all that I do. None of this happens without the support of family.

# About the Author

Dean M. Brenner is the president and founder of The Latimer Group and an expert in persuasive and powerful communication. He has coached executives, sales teams, business leaders, managers, and technical experts in a wide range of industries, on five continents.

*Sharing the Sandbox* is Dean's second book. His first title, *Move the World: Persuade Your Audience, Change Minds and Achieve Your Goals*, was published in 2007 by John Wiley & Sons.

In addition to his work with The Latimer Group, Dean has served since October 2004 as Chairman and Team Leader for the US Olympic Sailing Program. Since his appointment, Dean has led the organization through a period of great change, with dramatic growth in supporting athletes and significant changes in organizational culture. Dean led the team through the 2008 Games in Beijing and the 2012 Games in London.

Dean is also a well-decorated, Olympic-caliber sailor with seven national championships and five international team racing championships to his credit. He was a member of the US National Sailing Team for three years and placed second in the 2000 Olympic Selection Trials.

Dean earned an MBA in Finance from The Olin School of Business at Babson College; an MA in Shakespearean Literature from The University of Warwick, England; and a BA in English Literature and Government from Georgetown University. Prior to Georgetown, Dean attended The Kent School in Kent, Connecticut.

Dean was born in New York but grew up in Rhode Island. He now resides in Wallingford, Connecticut, with his wife, Emily, their son, Zachary, and their dog, Rowan.

*For more about Dean and The Latimer Group, please visit www.TheLatimerGroup.com. And for additional copies of* Sharing the Sandbox *or* Move the World, *please visit www.SharingTheSandbox.com.*

# Foreword

*By Kevin K. Cushing*

The word "team" is pervasive in our modern society. And all too often, the word and its true meaning are taken completely for granted.

We follow our favorite teams, we serve on project teams, we lead teams of volunteers… How many of our waking hours are *not* spent as part of a group where efforts or attitude impact each other? I submit that, for most of us, the correct answer is "very few." Among work, family, sports, faith and volunteerism, there are very few things in life that we attempt and accomplish in a solitary way.

But in my experience, "being on a team" is rarely a guarantee that you "have a team."

I've participated in recreational team sports since I was six, and I still play today, some fifty years later. Some teams clicked and others didn't. I've also been blessed to be a part of and lead teams in business for the last 40 years, from a 16-year-old supervisor to a business owner to my most recent role as CEO of AlphaGraphics, Inc. Almost all have been good or great experiences because of the character and commitment of the people involved.

But the concept of building great teams is a never-ending search for improvement, and this book will help that search. Dean Brenner gives all of us a great gift in *Sharing the Sandbox*, for this is not so much a book as it is a guide to how to become a better teammate and partner. It shows a path to a more fulfilling and balanced life.

Who among us doesn't aspire to have a bigger positive impact on those around us? We all do, and that is why I call this book a gift. It gives us a roadmap to close the gap between our current reality and a desired and better reality. Many of us suffer from "illusory superiority," which is a cognitive bias that causes us to overestimate our positive qualities and underestimate our negative ones. *Sharing the Sandbox* will help you assess what is *really* going on with your teams, and there is value throughout this book. Every chapter is a gem.

Dean Brenner's experiences—as a world-class competitive sailor, entrepreneur, and executive coach; and, for eight highly successful years, Chairman of the US Olympic Sailing Program—and his gift of insight and reputation as a straight shooter have come together in *Sharing the Sandbox*. He understands the dynamics of communications within a team setting better than anyone I know.

There are a lot of things to be learned from Dean Brenner. I realized this in our first meeting in 2007, which ultimately led to AlphaGraphics becoming the *only* company in the United States to be the title partner of a US National Olympic Team—the US Sailing Team AlphaGraphics. From the first time we met, it was obvious that Dean had a very practical and clear way of looking at the world, and this comes through loud and clear in *Sharing the Sandbox*. He lays out practical tools and methods and connects them with easily relatable examples. This book is 100 percent on the mark and 100 percent "Dean" in that it hits the target with little wasted effort, just like a champion athlete.

As I embark on the journey of the second half of my career, I look forward to carrying *Sharing the Sandbox* with me as a primary tool. I am certain that it will make me a better leader and teammate, and I am sure it will do the same for you as well.

Thank you, Dean.

*Kevin K. Cushing recently completed 22 years as the Chief Executive Officer of Alpha-Graphics, Inc. During Kevin's tenure, AlphaGraphics embarked on a highly successful and complete reinvention of its brand and its business. Kevin is widely recognized as a results-oriented, straight-shooting, team-oriented leader.*

## Author's Preface

The inspiration for the writing of this book did not come at a single, magical moment. This book has been a lifetime in the making, and I have drawn on the full scope of my life's experiences in this project. For better or for worse, when we work together, I bring everything I am into that moment. Within these pages, I write mostly as an executive coach and business owner, but often I am also writing as an athlete… a sports coach… a leader… a follower… a husband, father, son, and brother… and a friend. I bring the experiences of my full life to this book, and I think it makes the value deeper, for me and for you.

This approach makes life more honest and enjoyable, and it also creates unpredictable learning opportunities. We might be working together in a conference room on the 65th floor of a high rise in Singapore, and there might be a valuable idea that I learned racing sailboats 22 years ago in Watch Hill, Rhode Island. Or, I might remember what it was like to be relegated to the bench on my high school basketball team, and that might cause me to follow your leadership differently. Or, I may very well learn something valuable about communication from conversations with my young son, and that may impact the way I think about my work with you. I bring it all into my work, and I bring it all into this book.

I encourage you to adopt the same approach. As you read *Sharing the Sandbox*, think about all of your experiences, and about how they might make you a better teammate or partner. Think about all the ways you can apply what we discuss here. These concepts are not just about work. You can apply what we discuss here to almost anything.

The person who knows how to succeed within a team context possesses life's greatest skill. I believe that firmly, and I believe *Sharing the Sandbox* will give you lots to think about in your effort to be a better leader, manager, teammate and partner.

Good luck.

Wallingford, Connecticut
March 26, 2012

# Introduction: An Invitation to Be World Class

This book is about teams: how we build them, how we lead them, and how we succeed within them. Specifically, this book is about team communication and how we can use our words and our actions to bring together groups of people to create truly productive team experiences.

The business world's reliance on teams is constant. Our business culture is dominated by all kinds of them: project teams, cross-functional teams, virtual teams, global teams, boards. Teams are everywhere. We are expected to be able to contribute toward the good of them; if we seek advancement, we are expected to be able to lead them; and we are constantly judged by our ability to boost their productivity.

Let's start with a few simple but critical questions: Are you a good leader? Are you a good teammate? Do people follow your lead because they *want* to or because they *have* to? (Are you sure?) Do you want to have significant competitive advantage in the workplace? Perhaps a more important question is, Would others describe you as the great leader and teammate you think you are?

Whether you answer "Yes" or "No" to these questions, you'll have lots to think about as you read *Sharing the Sandbox*. The bottom line is this: Much of your success in the workplace is based on your ability to align and lead other people and to be productive within groups. This ability to "play well with others" is not easy to acquire; in fact, it's harder to do these days than ever before. But the principles of success are straightforward and easy to understand. *Sharing the Sandbox* will demystify the key elements of team success and provide a concrete roadmap of the route toward consistently positive team experiences for you and those around you.

The 21st century has changed the way we need to do things in so many ways. We have more access to information and more access to each other than ever before—and that trend is not changing any time soon. The net result? More and more people think they know enough to be in charge, everyone has an opinion, and everyone thinks the world needs to hear that opinion. We live in a constantly connected world, and we are inextricably linked to other people, all the time. The more informed and opinionated your population, the harder it is to lead—and the harder it is to align the people around you.

In *Sharing the Sandbox*, you will discover what is required to lead, support, build, and nurture teams; manage the people on those teams; and create entirely positive and productive team environments. You will learn that **being a good team leader or teammate is about three things:**

1. Your ability to contribute to the performance of the team

2. Your ability to observe the interests and needs of other team members and meet those needs and interests

3. Your ability to put the needs of other people before your own

*Sharing the Sandbox* is written as your guide to all things team, and we will look at teams of all kinds from a variety of angles and perspectives. *Sharing the Sandbox* is divided into three sections:

- In Part 1, we'll cover the fundamental issues of leadership, followership, and team communication. My goal in Part 1 is to help you take a close look at your own leadership and communication styles and to give you some important topics and concepts to think about.

- In Part 2, we will roll up our sleeves and get our hands dirty. We'll discuss specific tools, frameworks, and steps you can take to lead, manage, and participate on teams at a world-class level.

- And finally, in Part 3, we'll step back out to the big picture and conclude by posing some questions that have no easy answers but still require your thought and attention.[1]

---

[1]Throughout *Sharing the Sandbox*, I'll use these footnotes to give examples, tell stories, and otherwise digress. The main text will cover the primary content, and the footnotes will be where I roam around a bit, highlight a key point, or alert you to an upcoming quiz. Enjoy!

## The ARROW Metaphor

At the heart of *Sharing the Sandbox* is a simple metaphor that my colleagues at The Latimer Group and I call ARROW. Strong, functional teams are, above all else, *aligned*. The people on the team are working toward a common goal, and working together. If you represented each person on the team as an arrow on a piece of paper, all of the arrows would be pointing in the same general direction and, in some rare cases, *exactly* the same direction. When all the arrows are pointing in the same direction, the team is aligned and ready for success.

We've broken down the elements of alignment through the ARROW metaphor:

**A = R + R + O + W**

**A**lignment is the result of the following: clear **R**oles and Responsibilities, overt **R**espect among teammates, a strong sense of **O**wnership, and an undeniable **W**illingness to do the work. Each of the components of this equation is important. But only when we have all of them in place—plenty of understanding and agreement on roles and responsibilities, respect for the people around us, a strong sense of ownership, and a willingness to do the necessary work—only then do we have a shot at creating strong alignment.

## Who Is Sharing the Sandbox For?

This book is written for anyone who is, in some way, involved in a team. This book transcends industry or position on the organizational chart. This book is for anyone who has to work with others and wants to maximize the productivity and potential of teams they're part of. In other words, this book is for *you*. However, while it is for *you*, it is not *about* you. Instead, it is about the people around you and how you can be a good teammate to them.

This book is not a cheat sheet containing shortcuts to success. If you are good at what you do and are looking for ways to work effectively with others, if you are truly interested in learning more about how to be a good teammate, and if you are genuinely happy when you see others succeed, then *Sharing the Sandbox* will be a great resource for you.

I believe that the value of *Sharing the Sandbox* goes well beyond the professional world. Its principles can be applied to your participation in team sports regardless of your level of involvement. These principles can influence the way you coach and even the way you approach your relationships with friends and family. At their core, these principles are about how we interact with others and keep relationships productive, both at home and at work.

I'm the father of a young son. Watching our little Zachary grow up and learn the lessons of life is a joyful experience for me as a parent. But it is also an instructive one for an executive coach and student of people. In my observations, the lessons that are drilled into us as children all too often are forgotten by the time we enter the workplace. As professional adults, all of us, myself included, need a refresher on some of the things we teach our children: Share with the person next to you, treat acquaintances with kindness and respect, say thank you, and celebrate the successes of others. At its most elemental level, this book is about remembering that the key to being a great teammate is, first and foremost, about respect for those around us. This book is about learning to "share the sandbox" with our colleagues.[2]

It is my sincere hope that this book helps you become a stronger partner, teammate, leader, and manager of people. If we can harness the skills to become better teammates, if we can learn how to consistently build strong teams, if we can learn to take joy not just from our

---

[2]Not so long ago, my wife, Emily, and I hosted a birthday party for Zach's second birthday. This was your classic little-kid fete: tons of balloons, kids running around and playing, and lots of screaming little voices. You can picture it pretty clearly, I'm sure.

There is a transaction that takes place between little kids at these kinds of parties. The host child invites friends over for some great playtime, provides a little sugar high by way of a cake, and sends everyone home with a little goodie bag. In exchange, the birthday child gets to be the center of attention for a few hours and receives an outward show of affection. It's a pretty simple transaction: come to my house, bring me a gift, and sing to me, and I'll offer you a great time, all the cake you can eat, and a gift to take home.

Watching the kids and their parents at Zach's party reminded me that parents tirelessly give kids great advice on how to get along with other people. And that this great advice applies to people of any age. If only we adults could remember some of that same advice for ourselves…

own success but from the success of others and of the group, if we can learn to motivate people and cause them to *want* to work together, if we can learn to create an environment where human beings can thrive and succeed together, we will have perhaps the most-sought-after skills in the 21st century. We will have significant competitive advantage and create enormous value for ourselves and everyone around us.

Good luck!

# PART 1

## Fundamentals

THE LATIMER GROUP

# SHARING THE SANDBOX

> *"The first responsibility of the leader is to define reality.*
> *The last is to say, Thank you.*
> *In between, the leader is a servant."*
> **– Max DePree**

Each day of your professional life, you have a simple choice: Do you want people to work with you and follow your lead because they want to or because they have to? Think about your answer for a moment, because it is *the* fundamental question. Your answer will dictate almost every aspect of the way you partner with other people in the workplace. For those of you who choose the "want to" answer, you are in search of influence. You are in search of partnership and collaboration. You want people to want to work with you, and that's good.

On the other hand, for those of you who pause in your answer, or perhaps choose the "have to" answer, you do not seek influence. You are in search of something quite different—authority, plain and simple. You want to be in charge. You want people to just listen to you and do what you tell them to do. That's not always a bad thing, and, in fact, there are times when a simple, authoritative decision-making structure is a very *good* thing. But those are almost always times of crisis, and the authoritative leadership style is simply unsustainable over time. Eventually, an authoritarian approach wears thin, alienates those around you, and puts stress on the team environment.

I urge you to think carefully about the choice between influence and authority. The pursuit of influence is much harder. But it is a wonderful journey that leads toward new ways to collaborate and keeps us focused on finding common ground with other human beings. The pursuit of influence is one of constant understanding of other people and how we interact as human beings. The pursuit of authority can be easier, especially in the short term, but once you gain the authority you seek, it never lasts. Influence stands the test of time. Authority can evaporate quickly.

Most of us like to think that we are in pursuit of influence. Most of us like to think that people love working with us, that we are such dynamic people/leaders/partners/teammates that, obviously, everyone will want to partner with us. But most of us have a hard time looking in the mirror and seeing reality.[3] What we see in the mirror is rarely what everyone else sees.

Regardless of what you see in the mirror today, if you are legitimately interested in the pursuit of influence, then you are ready to take the necessary steps. Because being a great teammate, a great follower, and a great leader starts with the proper attitude. Why? Those concepts are rooted in your ability to care about the experiences of other people. They are about service to others, partnership with others. Being a great teammate is about *other people*.

We each have a style of doing things, certain behaviors that are typical for us. Being a great teammate is about first understanding the styles and behaviors of your teammates and, second, being willing, when appropriate, to calibrate your *own* comfortable behaviors to your teammates'.[4] Great teammates who are interested in gaining influ-

---

[3] QUIZ #1: Is your leadership style collaborative or authoritarian? (See quizzes at the end of Part 1.)

[4] Have you ever had a roommate? If so, then you have experienced the daily negotiations of being a teammate. You know what I'm talking about: those little compromises on whether the light stays on so you can read or the light goes off so your roommate can sleep, whether you stay up late watching a movie the night before your roommate has an important early morning meeting, whether the heat goes on or not. These daily compromises are great training for being a teammate. I'll be the first to admit that life can be easier without these little negotiations, but life can also be lonely without a roommate. I think that at some point, everyone should have to share a room with a sibling or a schoolmate—if only to learn how to get along well with others.

ence with those around them are willing to make compromises in their own behaviors out of respect for their fellow team members. Bad teammates are not. Bad teammates expect everyone else to adjust to them.

If we pursue influence, are we eschewing authority? Are influence and authority mutually exclusive? Of course not. Those with influence often end up with more than their fair share of authority as well. But that authority will, in large part, be based on their influence, which means it is based on respect, trust, and credibility. When we have influence, authority is usually close at hand. But if we pursue authority first and foremost, influence is rarely close by.

Do you want people to follow you because they want to or because they have to? Think about it—and keep thinking about it as you read this book. It is *the* fundamental question.

# SHARING THE SANDBOX

chapter 2: why some teams fail

*"Those who cannot remember the past are condemned to repeat it."*
**– George Santayana**

There are good teams and there are bad teams. Which do you prefer to be a part of? Me, too. Another question: When a team you are on fails, do you spend any time trying to figure out what happened? Or instead do you skulk away, trying to put the experience in your rearview mirror as quickly as possible? For the next few pages, let's not skulk away. Let's roll up our sleeves and dig in to the most common reasons why some teams fail to achieve success. Understanding the failures or shortcomings of other teams is at the heart of progress. So let's start there. Once we understand what can go wrong in a team environment, we can then build our teams on a stronger foundation.

I am fascinated by teams. This fascination began with my first real team experience, playing basketball in elementary school at St. Joseph's School in Bronxville, New York. I've lost touch with that community over the years, but I'll never forget the lessons I learned while playing ball for Coach Acolina and Coach Slattery, who preached that we kids should play together as a single unit. No matter which individual player scored the points, what mattered most was the success of the team as a whole. I think this resonated with me because, while I was a

good player, I was never the best. Recognizing that the team's achievement was more important than my own removed some of the weight
from my shoulders and certainly made me a better teammate. Perhaps
most importantly, though, this approach made the whole experience a
lot more fun, which showed me the value of the team construct. Team
victories were much more satisfying than personal ones. And when we
lost, sharing the disappointment with other teammates eased our individual burdens and strengthened our bonds. This experience taught
me to put the needs of a group before my own. I'd like to think I'm the
better for it.

Not all of my team experiences have been as positive as the one at
St. Joseph's. I've had more than my fair share of negative experiences,
but they have contributed equally to my approach and fascination with
teams. I can still remember the frustration when my high school senior-
year basketball team at The Kent School, stacked with returning talent,
underperformed all season. That team was pulled apart by cliques, dif-
fering agendas, and a total lack of alignment. It was easily the most
frustrating team experience of my life. I wasn't a major player on that
team. In fact, I rode the bench all season (and with good reason—I
wasn't very talented). But the bench gave me a front row seat to see
what a bad team experience could look like.

What happened? Lots of classic symptoms of a bad team dynamic
were there.[5]

First, we had lots of guys who felt they deserved playing time, and
there was an obvious competitive dynamic before the season even
started. Some of that can be good if it is channeled in a good way. But
our "team" seemed to keep forgetting that we were actually supposed
to be playing together. We had team members openly rooting against
the success of those on the floor at the time, hoping someone else's
mistakes would lead to more playing time for them. Second, we had

---

[5]Here's a little more background on this team. We returned nearly every member of the prior year's team, which
was good, but not great. We also added several new players to the mix. We had tons of experience and talent. We
had played pickup together all fall, and everyone knew each other well. Our coaching staff was experienced. And
yet, despite all of these things, we ended the year with almost exactly the same record as the previous year. Based
on our experience and our talent, I think all of us were expecting a much better result than the previous season.

multiple "teams within the team." So when things started to fall apart, people retreated to their cliques and the team fractured. Finally, we had leadership (coaches and one or two leading players) who saw all of this happening and did nothing about it.[6]

When a team is good, it's a great experience. But when a team is bad, it's worse than ugly. Successful teams are capable of remarkably high productivity, accomplishment, and satisfaction for all involved. Failed teams, however, represent underachievement, wasted resources, and utter frustration. If you can apply the steps needed to create successful teams, you will own the key to the castle of organizational success. This book offers that key.

In order to get the key, though, you must first understand why most teams fail to achieve their goals. And to understand *that*, we must take a step back and look at what a team really is.

Quite simply, a team is a collection of individuals. Since each of us is unique, each combination of people has a different dynamic. Change out just one person on a team, and you have an entirely new team, a new organism that needs to be understood for what it is: something unique.

Ah, but then you might ask, "What if we don't change the personnel on the team and instead reassemble a team that has been successful in the past? Isn't that new team really the same old team?" Probably not. Why? There is a simple answer: Things change. Since their last project together, the team members have evolved, and furthermore, they now face a new assignment. The challenges of the latest project will likely elicit different behaviors than earlier ones did. These behaviors will create a different set of issues for the team. Think of it this way: A team is like a living organism whose cells are constantly mutating.

The big problem with this is that we live in a world that values repeatable outcomes. We constantly seek efficiency, process, and rules to

---

[6]It's interesting to me that almost 25 years later, I still think about this team and the opportunity lost. The coaches or any of several players on the team could have solved these problems, if we had only dealt with them directly. But none of us did, myself included. We all just "whistled past the graveyard," either hoping the problems would solve themselves or perhaps just not caring either way. I suppose therein lies the negative power of the underperforming team: The season might end, but the frustration and lessons learned linger for a lifetime.

create these outcomes. We want to learn what works, and then relent-lessly perform it over and over again. But you know what? That concept is very hard to apply to team building and team leading. Every situation is different, and it is nearly impossible to take the exact same techniques that worked with one team and use them with another.

Luckily, there are some best practices that can be applied consistently, and we'll look at all of them, especially in Part 2. But first, let's kick off our discussion of what *does* work with a discussion of what *does not* work. Let's take a look at the most common reasons why teams fail. When we understand the most common causes of failure, we are on the path to discovering the causes of success.

There are many issues that can contribute to a poor team experience. But these 10 are the most common and, I believe, the most fundamental. By discussing these 10 issues, we not only highlight the characteristics of bad teams, but we also lay the groundwork for a discussion of what makes a great team.

1.  **No alignment of goals.** This is a theme that will recur throughout this book. Great teams need, first and foremost, something to work toward. They need goals: a point on the map that they are moving toward and the common purpose that has brought them all together. Without clear goals, the team will start to drift apart, wither, and die, even when the members of the team enjoy each other's company. A lack of goals will reduce motivation, interest, and involvement, and the entire team construct falls apart. In our coaching work with the clients of The Latimer Group, the unsuccessful teams we encounter almost always have a lack of clear goals at the root of their issues.[7]

2.  **No alignment of the plan, commitment, or behaviors.** Alignment around some clear goals is required, but there is more. We also need alignment around three things that will

---

[7] If you are highlighting key concepts in this book, take note of the concept "create alignment." It's going to come up a lot, and it is Key Concept #1. We'll summarize all these key concepts at the end of Part 1.

contribute to the team's ability to meet its goals: the plan to achieve the goals, the expected commitment level, and the necessary behaviors. If we don't agree on the plan, the commitment, and the behaviors, then having goals is meaningless. Goals are required, but so is an agreement about how we will reach the goals.

3. **No sense of ownership.** The great investor Warren Buffett once said, "No one washes a rental car." In other words, we care about the things we own much more than the things we rent or borrow. No one paints a rented house. But once you own that house, the behaviors toward that house change dramatically. You care a great deal more about the property. So, too, with your teams and the projects they are working on. If your team consists of people just "punching the clock," not really caring about the outcome, you are guaranteed to have a bad team experience. The team will underperform. We need to find a way to cause the people on the team to care about the outcome, to "own" it.[8]

4. **A one-size-fits-all attitude toward team members.** The great UCLA basketball coach John Wooden was often accused of giving his star players, like Lew Alcindor (now known as Kareem Abdul-Jabbar), special treatment. Wooden's attitude toward this accusation has always fascinated me. He embraced the fact that he did, in fact, treat people differently. Wooden preached that everyone is different, and each needs different things. Why, then, would he treat everyone exactly the same way? Now, there are some things that should apply to all members of the team. Everyone should have the same opportunities for salary increases and benefits. Everyone is entitled to the same level of professional respect. There are many things that can, and should, apply to all. But beyond those things, people should be treated differently. Some people are more produc-

---

[8]Key Concept #2: Create ownership.

tive when they are pushed hard. Some people are more productive when they are left alone. Some people need an extra
pat on the back. Others don't. Some not only accept negative
feedback but actually *want* to hear it. Everyone is different, and
understanding what each person on your team needs to be
productive is at the heart of a flexible leadership style. People
are not the same, and trying to treat everyone as if they were is
a recipe for underperformance.

5.  **Rigid application of the lessons of the past.** Here's some-
    thing I hear all the time: "Well, this has always worked for me,
    so I'm going to keep doing it." On the surface, this is reason-
    able. But when we apply this to team behaviors, it falls apart
    pretty quickly. If we accept the earlier premise that every team
    situation is different, then, by extension, we have to adopt a
    flexible approach toward team leadership and participation.
    Just because something worked before, with a different team
    and under different circumstances, doesn't mean it will work
    this time. It might work—but it might not.[9]

6.  **Dysfunctional or insufficient communication.** When my col-
    leagues and I work with dysfunctional teams to find the issues
    that are causing problems, we find that "communication" is al-
    most always one of them. People need to believe that they can
    discuss issues openly and honestly.[10] When the lines of com-
    munication are closed or cloudy, team members believe they

---

[9]Key Concept #3: Be flexible.

[10]I was involved with an organization at one point, as a board member, where the executive director preached "good communication." But there were whispers that this preaching was not practiced in the office. I once dropped by unannounced and found the executive director in his office with the door closed. The assistant told me he was not to be disturbed. I asked if he was in a meeting or on the phone. He wasn't. "He likes his private time," she explained. That's fine in moderation. But upon further inspection, we learned that this was his standard operating procedure and that he would spend hours a day in his office with the door closed, not to be disturbed. It created a closed, withdrawn communication dynamic in the office that trickled down to everyone. The leader was sending a message of "leave me alone," which affected the entire office experience. He wasn't there much longer.

have no outlet, and when a person has no outlet, stress builds up and the team dynamic deteriorates.[11]

7. **Leadership's unwillingness to eliminate a bad performer.** Great teams have a certain DNA strain that makes them productive and allows them to perform at a high level. Members of great teams push each other to excel, and everyone on the team is motivated by the belief that everyone else on the team also wants to perform at a high level. But when one or two members of the team are less interested in performing well, or when their performance just can't keep up with the rest of the team, the leader has two choices: try to rehabilitate the situation or eliminate the bad performer.[12] Every situation is different, and oftentimes an attempt at rehabilitation is appropriate, but at some point, leadership must pick the second choice: Make a change. And if leadership is unwilling to do so, it can have a severe impact on the morale and motivation of the rest of the team. Sometimes change is unavoidable.

8. **A holier-than-thou leadership attitude.** Nothing hurts motivation on the team more quickly than leadership that holds itself to standards that are different than everyone else's.[13] Leadership must exemplify the behaviors and commitment it expects from the rest of the team and needs to demonstrate that it is willing to do the same things that are expected of others.[14]

---

[11]Key Concept #4: Open the lines of communication.

[12]What defines a bad performer? Lots of things. Perhaps the person does not respect the roles of others or doesn't treat others with respect. Perhaps the person just does their own job poorly. Perhaps the person does their job well, but lacks any chemistry with others and ends up being a distraction. There are lots of ways to define a bad performer. The important point here is that when you have bad performance, in any one of its many forms, you need to either try to rehabilitate the situation or make a change. And good leaders cannot be afraid to make that change.

[13]Key Concept #5: Practice what you preach.

[14]I learned this lesson the hard way at an early age. My dad was a good dad in a lot of ways, and I owe him a great deal. But he ran a household that clearly had different rules for different people. He was an old-school, "do as I say, not as I do" kind of guy. I recognized this at a very young age, and it had a major impact on me. In the 21st century, leadership has to, absolutely has to, practice what it preaches. Anything less than that will almost certainly become toxic within your team.

9. **Disengaged leadership.** Great teams care about the performance and the success of the team. And this is directly tied to the care displayed by leadership. When team leadership cares about the outcome and shows it, the team is more likely to care about the outcome also. When leadership does not care, no one else will, either. Great teams care about the outcome. Leadership *has* to care and has to *show* that it cares.

10. **Lack of respect and trust.** Perhaps the sum total of everything in this chapter is represented by the twin concepts of respect and trust. Good teams have them. Bad teams don't. People on good teams trust that everyone else is going to get their job done, and everyone treats each other with respect. People on bad teams don't. Distrust and disrespect become toxic and filter through a team, with terminal consequences.

One of the best ways to describe the difference between good teams and bad teams is this: Good teams don't waste any competitive energy focused inwardly at others on the team. Bad teams do. Good teams are aligned, have ownership, good communication, good leadership, trust, and respect. And because they have all these things, the members of these good teams can point their competitive energy outwardly at the competition or the task at hand. With the energy channeled where it belongs, outwardly at the competition, a successful outcome is far more likely. Bad teams do not have any of these things; they end up wasting energy and time and creating stress.

# SHARING THE SANDBOX

chapter 3: 21st century realities that cannot be ignored

*"Never confuse activity for achievement."*
– John Wooden

One of most frequently overlooked facts about team building today is this: The realities of the 21st century have fundamentally changed the way we build, manage, and lead teams. The result of this new dynamic is that being an effective teammate or team leader is harder than ever. Not only do we have to learn new skills, but we also have to *unlearn* outdated skills that may have contributed to past success.

Plenty has been written about the rapidly changing world in which we live. It's no secret that our world has undergone, and continues to undergo, significant change and evolution—technologically, economically, and politically. The world looks a lot different now than it did even 10 years ago.

*Sharing the Sandbox* isn't the place to catalog, debate, and discuss all the changes that have occurred. But it should include those new realities that are relevant to our discussion:

1.  **We have nearly unlimited access to information and to each other.** People feel like they can learn almost anything they want about a topic or a person, and they are correct. Those who want to know more about a topic can easily and

readily find it. People have the option of being better informed than at any other time in history. Regardless of whether the average person actually *is* better informed, what's important is that the average person *thinks* he or she is better informed than people used to be. Furthermore, people feel they should have unlimited access to *you*—and unless you resist, they will *get* unlimited access.[15]

2.  **Everyone has an opinion, on almost everything.** The constantly connected world of the Internet and social media gives the average person the sense that his or her opinions matter, and they now have public forums in which to share those opinions broadly and quickly. While the possession of opinions is not new for human beings, social media and reality television have caused many to believe that their opinions are more important than they really are. People use social media channels for a variety of things from sharing photos of their kids or pets to telling everyone who will listen what they are doing at that exact moment to sharing their opinions, subtle or otherwise, on everything from sports to religion to politics. It seems that everyone has an opinion he or she thinks is worth sharing and thinks his or her life and what he or she is doing at that moment is of the utmost importance.

3.  **People change jobs and industries much more often than ever before.** This not only means that we need a broader array of skills, but it also means we need to know how to bet-

---

[15]My wife, Emily, teaches at a top New England boarding school. Here's a true story that has happened several times over the years. Our home phone rings, I pick it up, and there is a student of Emily's on the line. Here's the typical exchange:

Student: "Can I speak to Mrs. Brenner, please?"

Me: "She's not available right now."

Student: "But I really need to speak with her."

Me: "OK, but she can't speak right now. Send her an e-mail, and she'll respond."

Student: "I already did, and she hasn't responded yet."

Me: "How long ago did you send the e-mail?"

Student: "10 minutes ago."

Me: (stunned silence....)

ter deal with people. If we were to spend our entire career in the same company or even the same industry (as many of our grandparents or parents did), we would experience exposure to a much narrower profile of skills and personalities in our colleagues. Instead, we experience people who have done different things, worked in different industries, lived in different cities, and almost certainly grew up somewhere else. This means that the people we deal with will bring different perspectives and sensibilities to their work with us.

4. **Teams are more global, virtual, and remote than ever before.** How do we lead and partner with people who grew up in different cultures, with different academic training, and with different native languages than our own? And how do we deal with those issues without seeing our teammates face-to-face more than once or twice a year? The global, virtual economy makes team building very challenging. (We'll deal with the challenges of global teams more specifically in chapter 15 of *Sharing the Sandbox*.)

These realities present a challenging new environment for team leaders. Why? Because many people walk into the room thinking they know as much as the person in charge and, with an inflated sense of self, are convinced that they should be consulted on all sorts of things. Your job as the 21st-century leader requires that you embrace these realities and be prepared to deal with them. And in addition, you'll need to know how to deal with many more kinds of people, personalities, and behavior patterns than has any prior generation of business professionals.

Building consensus in a harmonious way within these new realities is difficult. If you pursue harmony and ask for lots of input and opinions, decision making will take a long time. What's more, this so-called design-by-committee approach will produce a lot of "camels" (allegorically speaking, the product of a failed group effort to design a horse).

On the other hand, if you choose to pursue an efficient decision-making process, you may end up with motivation issues and disgruntled team members. Regardless of the details of the situation, nearly everyone will have an opinion on what they would do differently if they were in charge.

How should effective 21st-century leaders deal with these realities? A few things come to mind:

1. **Start by acknowledging and internalizing the existence of these new realities.** Ignore them at your own leadership peril. Once we embrace their existence, we can then begin to build strategies to deal with these realities.

2. **Make conscious choices on your team's norms and behaviors.** What kinds of behaviors do you want the people on your team to exhibit? And, specifically, how will you bring those behaviors to life? Team building shouldn't be taken lightly in any environment, especially in the 21st century. You need to care about the dynamic of your team. You need to care about your communication norms. You need to make conscious choices on the types of behaviors and norms you want on your team and then work hard to bring those to life.

3. **Different scenarios call for different modes.** In a crisis, you don't have time to ask for everyone's opinion. Shrink your circle of advisors and start making some decisions. In calmer times with less pressure, take advantage of the extra time to use a different approach that allows for collaboration. And, regardless of the mode you set for the team, communicate what mode you are in and why.

4. **Always remember that leadership is not a popularity contest.**[16] Do the best you can, communicate what you are doing and why, and simply accept the fact that not everyone will always like what you are doing. Some will think they can do better, and maybe they are correct. When it's their turn to lead, they'll get their chance. But in the moment, be self-assured

---

[16]Here's a great Winston Churchill quote: "So, you've got some enemies? That's good. That means you have stood up for something in your life."

that you are in charge and lead through confident decision making rather than the desire to be everyone's best friend.

I once led a workshop on executive leadership communication skills with one of our top clients. Spending two days working with the executives in that large organization was a great opportunity to discuss real-world challenges that leaders are facing.

One of the participants brought up a great point during the session. He said, "I always thought I had good communication skills, but lately, the feedback has been less positive. I don't think I'm doing anything differently." We discussed at length and the conclusion was a simple one. He was correct: He was *not*, in fact, doing anything differently—and that was the problem. What worked in 1992 or 2002 doesn't necessarily work in 2012.

There is one more 21st-century reality worth mentioning in this chapter. In our current market environment, where every expense is scrutinized, where every sale takes painstaking effort, and where jobs are constantly at risk, business success can be highly elusive. Every organization needs its people producing more efficiently and at a higher level than ever before. Each of us is being asked to give a little more, often for no additional compensation. Yet, at exactly the time when organizations need their people producing at a higher level, budgets for professional development are being cut. The message seems to be, "We need you to be better, but we have no resources to help you get there."

One might think that the lack of professional development could be offset by increased internal mentoring from more-senior people in the organization. Well, if your organization needs you to be producing at a higher level, they are probably putting the same pressure, if not more, on the people above you. This means that internal responsibilities like mentoring may not be a priority.

This reality means that the teams and team leaders out in the field and sprinkled throughout each organization are, to a certain degree, on their own to set themselves up, learn what they need to learn, and make decisions. They resemble the military field commander who is expected to win but without any guidance from headquarters.

The good news? For that team leader, line manager, or business executive who really wants to be better, there are resources like *Sharing the Sandbox*. The bad news is that you have to seek improvement yourself; you have to want to go above and beyond to grow.[17]

One final thought: I urge each of you to remember that information is not knowledge, and knowledge is not judgment.[18] Success starts with information, but knowledge and, eventually, judgment are also required. That has not changed, and I submit that it never will. We have more access to information than ever before, but that does not guarantee us any additional knowledge or judgment.

The bottom line is that we live in a world that is constantly reinventing itself, and it is doing so at breakneck speed. As leaders and followers, we need to be looking for ways to do the same if we want to be productive members of great teams.

---

[17] More from Winston Churchill: "The most important thing about education is the appetite." In our context here, the point is that if you are not interested in growing as a leader or a teammate, resources like executive coaching or team-building workshops or books like *Sharing the Sandbox* won't help you very much. You have to want to improve before anything else is possible.

[18] I'm paraphrasing and expanding on both Albert Einstein ("information is not knowledge") and Frank Zappa ("information is not knowledge, and knowledge is not wisdom").

# SHARING THE SANDBOX

chapter 4: goals, tasks, and control

*A goal without a plan is just a wish.*
**– Antoine de Saint-Exupery**

I trained for six years, as part of a team of three, to qualify for the 2000 US Olympic Sailing Team. We had some initial success, but after a couple of years of great effort, we were generally not getting the results we wanted. After trying everything, we made some marginal gains, but our growth had essentially stalled. Then, with 18 months until the national Olympic selection trials, we decided to spend some time with Jerry May, who was the US Sailing Team sports psychologist at the time. My teammates and I trekked up to Jerry's place in the mountains of northern California and spent three days literally and figuratively sitting on his couch, trying to figure out what was wrong with our team.

Jerry asked us what sorts of things we thought about and were focused on as a team. All of our answers were centered on lofty team performance goals. As he dug deeper, there was lots of discussion about making the Olympic team, marching in the opening ceremony, winning a medal, standing on the podium, hearing our national anthem. We had lots to talk about there.

But then Jerry asked us to go beyond our goals, and he started to ask us about the tasks we would need to accomplish to meet our goals.

We had some things to talk about, but the conversation was much shorter, much less specific. Jerry quickly pointed out that this was our problem. We were overly focused on our goals and not focused enough on the tasks necessary for us to achieve them.

In Jerry's words, we were almost completely "goal oriented" when we needed to be much more "task oriented." Goals are a great thing to have, Jerry told us. They are a requirement for success. But once you know what the goals are, you should essentially put them up on a shelf. Every once in a while, you should pull them down, dust them off, make sure they still work for you, and use them to get re-motivated. But after that, they should go back up on the shelf. Your daily focus should be on the steps necessary to reach those goals.

Understanding the difference between being goal oriented and being task oriented was a breakthrough for our team, and it has had a profound impact on my professional life. It is also a critical theme in this book.[19] In our work at The Latimer Group, we always discuss with our clients the importance of goals. But then we encourage clients to move beyond those goals and get specific about the tasks required for success. This is exactly what successful teams do. Goals are great, and they are critical to your success. But if you focus exclusively on a goal, something far off in the future, you may end up stumbling on the essential steps required to get there.

Now let's take the concept a step further. How do we know the tasks on which to focus? To find the answer, we will look once again to the world of sailing.

In any competitive endeavor, there are things we can control and things we cannot. Strong competitors devote most of their energy to managing the factors that are within their control. Weaker competitors often end up wasting energy and focus on things that are beyond their control.[20]

---

[19]Key Concept #6: Balance goals with tasks.

[20]There are two things we all can always control when we are on a team: our effort and our attitude. We can always give the endeavor everything we have, and we can always have a positive attitude and treat our teammates with respect. It's amazing how many adults miss this.

In sailing, there are several things within your control: Your team has to be prepared to race. The members of your team need to be rested, strong, and hydrated. The boat and sails need to be clean, well maintained, and totally functional. You need to know how to use your equipment to sail as fast as possible. There are many things in sailing that are completely within your control.

However, there are also things that are important to your success but are well beyond your control: What will the wind or weather do? How prepared is your competition?[21] What decisions will the race committee make in administering the races? Once we embrace the concept of being task oriented, how do we decide which tasks should come first? A great way to filter through the priority of tasks is by using the concept of "control." Start by focusing on the tasks that you can have an impact on. Control the controllable first.[22] Think about the things that are beyond your control later.

If something is beyond your control, should it be ignored? I don't think so. Obsessing on the uncontrollable is a bad idea, but so is ignoring the uncontrollable. Once a variable or a task has been identified, even if the outcome cannot be controlled, great teams and great team leaders will at least think about a decision-making process for dealing with new information as it becomes available.

The best sailors in the world have many types of skills. But, as with great teams, great sailors have similar DNA. First, they control the things that are controllable: Their boat is always ready to go; the sailors are prepared, rested, and strong; and they know how to make the boat go as fast as possible. And second, while they acknowledge that there are things beyond their control, they do not obsess about these things (although they do not ignore them, either). The best sailors essentially make a compromise with themselves. They identify the variables that are uncontrollable and design a plan for making decisions on those

---

[21] To quote the great Mickey Rivers (philosopher king and 1970s-era centerfielder for the New York Yankees): "Ain't no sense worryin' about the things you got control over, 'cause if you got control over 'em, ain't no sense worryin'. And ain't no sense worryin' about the things you got no control over, 'cause if you got no control over 'em, ain't no sense worryin." Um… well said?

[22] Key Concept #7: Control the controllable.

things.[23] While they cannot control such elements as the wind and the weather, they make themselves as well informed as possible, and they divide the responsibilities up among the team so that the group as a whole is ready to make consistently good decisions when new information presents itself.

Here's a simple summary: *Good teams consistently prepare themselves to be successful.* Teams that have goals and well-understood tasks—who are well organized, have great attitudes, and have some talent—are consistently going to be in a position to succeed. And, as Jerry told my team years ago, if we consistently put ourselves in a position to succeed, we'll win more than our fair share. The focus should not be on the end result. The focus should always be on preparing, constructing the team, and giving yourself the opportunity to succeed.

There is one word to describe a team that has positioned itself to be successful: *aligned*. That's our ultimate goal when we are building a team. We want a team of people who are aligned in all ways: their skills, their goals, their efforts, their attitudes—everything.

So how did the story with Jerry end? It got both worse *and* better. Jerry got us focused on the proper things and our results did improve, but eventually some changes had to be made. We just could not get total alignment within the team, and eventually some personnel changes were unavoidable. The final evolution of the team achieved greater heights than we had ever enjoyed before, but in the end, we fell short of our final goal and narrowly missed qualifying for the 2000 US Olympic Sailing Team.

We'll come back to the concept of alignment later, in chapter 10.

---

[23]Key Concept #8: Plan for the uncontrollable.

# SHARING THE SANDBOX

chapter 5: great communication skills

*When you stand on the stage, you must have a sense that you are addressing the whole world, and that what you have to say is so important that the whole world must listen.*

**– Stella Adler**

Have you ever been in the company of one of those rare souls who can clearly articulate a point? Have you ever met that person who can artfully harness a meeting by clearly stating what the group is struggling to express? Have you ever seen that person who walks onstage and absolutely owns the room the moment they open their mouth?

I've met people like this a few times in my life. And when you watch and listen to someone with these types of skills, it's something special to see and hear. When we are in the presence of someone like this, we tend to remember the moment, their name, and what they are talking about. The rest of the people we listen to tend to fade into the background noise, exiting our consciousness as quickly as they entered it.

Great communication in the modern business world, therefore, requires that the speaker think about being memorable. Think about this: When you speak, how easy do you make it for your team or your audience to remember what you say? In the 21st century, it's critical to prepare and structure your message so that you make it easy for your audience to remember what you say; otherwise, you risk quickly fading from memory. There is simply too much information coming at each of us every day. Make it easy for your audience. Your audience will benefit and so will you.[24]

No book on team building and team communication would be complete without at least some mention of the importance of communication skills. We can have all the book knowledge on leadership, followership, and teams, and we can be prepared to take all the necessary steps, but if we lack the ability to communicate persuasively, we are destined to fall short of our goals.

Are you persuasive?[25] When you speak and write, do you have the ability to persuade people to do what you want them to do and to believe what you want them to think? Think carefully before you answer this one, because in my experience, precious few people have this skill at their fingertips. I'll submit that the power to persuade is, as David McCullough writes, power indeed. The people who can use their words and their actions to persuade others to buy their product, follow their lead, invest in their idea, or adopt their strategy have a powerful competitive advantage. Those with the power to persuade are in demand. People want to be on their teams. People follow their lead. Persuasive people tend to get noticed, heard, remembered, and, eventually, promoted.

Communication is always important, but especially so when you are the leader of an organization. Leadership communication must be able to withstand extra scrutiny and has to go above and beyond the normal level of good communication. All leadership communication must have a purpose and an intended impact. Followers and listeners will pick up every nuance of the communication. People will hold you to a higher standard than others. They will parse your words, looking for your true intentions. They will dissect your communication and dis-

---

[24]Key Concept #9: Be memorable.

[25]QUIZ #2: How well do you prepare to communicate? (See quizzes at the end of Part 1.)

cuss not *whether it could have been* better, but specifically *how it should have been better.* If you are a leader within your organization, or aspire to become one, can your communication skills stand up to that level of scrutiny? They need to, because if they don't, your lack of good communication skills will eventually impact your career path.

My colleagues and I at The Latimer Group have done a good deal of writing, speaking, and blogging about this topic, and I've even written a book about it.[26] We are well aware that persuasive communication is not easy. It takes plenty of thought, planning, and practice. But the concepts that lead to persuasive communication are pretty straight-forward. Here are five of the most important. If put these into practice, they will help you immediately.

1.  **Have a clear goal every time you speak.** What do you want your audience to think or do when you are done speaking? If you start with a clear goal for your communication opportunity, your preparation will be quicker and of better quality. Set a clear goal for yourself, and then focus all of your preparation on helping yourself achieve that goal. Only when you know your desired destination does it become possible to get where you want to go.

2.  **Spend time thinking about the needs and desires of your audience.** Before designing the agenda for a meeting, for instance, spend some time thinking about the current mindset of your audience. What will cause them to say "yes" or "no" to your requests? Too many of us communicate from an egocentric place. Don't spend all your time thinking about what you want to say. Spend most of your time thinking about the issues your audience will care about. When you do this, you will be more likely to design a message that will persuade them, and you also will show them the respect they deserve.[27]

---

[26] *Move the World: Change Minds, Persuade Your Audience, and Achieve Your Goals* was published in 2007 and is available at www.SharingTheSandbox.com.

[27] Consider this quote from Franklin Delano Roosevelt: "Remember that you are just an extra in everyone else's play." In other words, it's not all about you. Walk a mile in the other person's shoes, and you are preparing to communicate in a respectful, audience-centric way.

3. **Make the benefits to your audience the common denominator to every aspect of your message.** Do you want to persuade someone of something? Then make the benefits the highlight of the message. If your message lacks clear benefits, you will struggle to persuade anyone of anything.

4. **Be authentic and sincere.** When you deliver your message, don't worry too much about how you stand, where you put your hands, how you cock your head, or how many jokes you should tell in your opening. Those things do matter, but what matters most is your confidence to be yourself. Just be authentic. When you stand up to speak, speak in your own voice and with your own style. Do it your way, just as if you were speaking to a friend.[28]

   Equally important, be sincere. When you stand up to speak, show the audience that you care about the topic. To quote presidential speechwriter James Hume, who wrote for seven presidents: Preparation begins "the moment you start caring. Only then are you ready to speak to an audience. Because an audience can be convinced only when they see you care about what you are discussing."

5. **Practice.** Acquiring any new skill requires many things, coaching and instruction among them. If you want to become a better baseball player, acquiring new knowledge and finding a good coach are important steps. But without sufficient practice, all the books and coaching in the world won't make you better. The same goes for communication. Many of our client companies ask us to quantify The Latimer Group's value to them, asking, "Can you guarantee communication improvements?" Guarantees are a fool's game. We guarantee the transfer of knowledge and good tools and frameworks. But unless the person we are coaching makes a commitment to improve-

---

[28]Remember the advice of presidential speechwriter Peggy Noonan: "Be you, try to be honest, speak with all the candor you can muster, and say it the way you'd say it to your family."

ment, any guarantee we might provide is worthless. There are no magic bullets, no get-rich-quick schemes, no lose-100-pounds-in-100-days ploys. The amount you practice will determine your success.[29]

When you do all these things, you are simply increasing the chances that you will connect with your audience, and when you do that, you make it more valuable for them and more likely that you will enjoy a successful meeting, phone call, or presentation.

One of the key elements of your success as a leader is your ability to get groups of people to move together toward a common goal. How can you achieve that without being able to communicate in a clear and powerful way?

Finally, always remember that great communication skills are not one way. Great communication is also about listening, absorbing what has been delivered, and reflecting back what you have heard into your next communication. Your leadership communication should only be focused on the outbound, from you to the audience. You should focus on the inbound as well and listen to what others are telling you.

Do you want to become a better leader or teammate? Spend some time examining your own communication skills.

---

[29]The great golfer Ben Hogan once said, "Golf is a game of luck. The more I practice, the luckier I get." Exactly.

# SHARING THE SANDBOX

chapter 6: fingerprints

*All our knowledge has its origins in our perceptions.*
**– Leonardo da Vinci**

About 10 years ago, before I founded The Latimer Group, I worked for a great guy (and still a good friend) named Bill. He leads a management consulting firm that is headquartered in Connecticut and has a national presence. While working there, I picked up on a great concept that I have adapted to our work at The Latimer Group: the concept of "fingerprints."[30]

Every time we touch something, we leave fingerprints behind. Each set of prints is unique and, as such, is proof of our individual presence in a particular place. Each time we interact with someone, we leave behind figurative fingerprints. *These* fingerprints comprise the unique impressions, perceptions, and a lasting impact we leave on everyone and everything with which we interact. The way we treat people, the way we speak, and the way we conduct ourselves all leave a lasting impact. This applies to every one of us. And since teams are nothing more than collections of individuals, then it is true for all organizations as well.

---

[30]Hearty thanks to Bill, who not only founded and leads a highly successful consulting practice, but also has been a friend and mentor since the first days of The Latimer Group.

We all become known for something—our personal or organizational brand, if you will. We leave our figurative fingerprints everywhere we go.

Once we understand this reality, it is an easy leap to say that business leaders—and strong teams—must give some thought to what they want their individual and collective fingerprints to be. Forward-thinking, sophisticated teams make conscious decisions ahead of time on how they want to be perceived by others. This is critical to creating well-aligned, successful, and effective organizations and teams. The more thought we put into this concept, the more we can control the way we are perceived and the brand image that we leave behind. We can decide how we want to be known; we can decide how we want to be remembered.

We'll come back to this concept later in the book when we discuss in greater detail how we actually construct strong teams.[31] But for now, I simply want you to think about the fingerprints, individual or organizational, that you leave behind all the time. Think about the impressions you and your team leave on others. Is your team perceived the way you want it to be? Are you sure? If you are building a new team, you have the luxury of planning and choosing the members of your team based on whether they are likely to leave behind the fingerprints you want your team to have.

Let me illustrate the point with some actual organizational fingerprints. At The Latimer Group, we have five impressions that we strive to leave on every interaction:

1. **Thought leadership.** We pursue constant evolution and improvement of our communication frameworks, methods, and tools. We strive to be relevant. We strive to be aware of the general business climate and resultant needs and demands on communication skills.

---

[31] Finding the correct people to have on your team requires examination of lots of different things, from the hard skills that will make them effective in your endeavor, to the way they treat people, to the way they represent your organization, to the way they actually do their work. There are many ways to look at whether people fit on your team, and we'll look at all of them.

2. **Collaboration.** We believe that the creative process is best served and problems are best solved in a collaborative environment. We work *with* our clients, not around them or for them. We don't solve our clients' problems for them. We work with them to identify the path to success, and then we coach them to solve their problems for themselves. In other words, we won't do your important, year-end sales presentation for you. But we'll stand right there with you and help you put on the best possible performance. At the end of the day, the performance is yours, but we'll be with you every step of the way. That's a big difference.[32]

3. **Simplicity.** We distill issues and concepts down to their essence. Our clients are busy, successful executives and professionals. A significant aspect of our value added should be our ability to present concepts in ways that are memorable, digestible, and easy to put into action. In addition, our value added should also include our ability to provide clients with simple tools and frameworks that will help them solve problems for themselves in an efficient manner.

4. **Authenticity.** We believe people communicate best when they are authentic. So we encourage everyone we interact with to speak in their own voices and with their own styles. We don't hold up some ideal and say, "Just do it like this person." Rather, we want our clients to develop the confidence to be themselves. The reason? Authenticity is a form of honesty, and having honest relationships with your own clients will pave the way for your success.[33]

---

[32]Key Concept #10: Collaborate. We live in a permanent state of interdependence and connectedness. Success today requires successful interaction with other people, which means our ability to effectively collaborate with the people around us is now a mission-critical skill.

[33]Key Concept #11: Encourage authenticity. At its most elemental level, authenticity is really about honesty. It takes confidence to be comfortable being yourself. It also takes trust in the people around you. Confidence and trust are, in many ways, two sides of the same coin, and that coin buys you the ability to be authentic. When we are authentic, we are showing our true self to those around us. This makes us more compelling and interesting—and more likely to bring out that same authenticity in others. When we show our authentic self to others (and encourage others to do the same), we build a high level of trust within the team. In other words, accept people as they are, and ask others to do the same for you.

5. **Positive—but honest—reinforcement.** Our ultimate value is driven by our ability to coach better communication skills. We believe in building people up rather than tearing them down. In other words, we coach in a positive way. However, when brutal honesty is required, we do not avoid it.[34] For some people, coaching is a way of showing others that they know more than everyone else. For us, coaching is about serving the client. In the words of NBA coach John Wooden, "A coach is someone who can give correction without causing resentment."

These are The Latimer Group's organizational fingerprints, and I share them with you in the hope that you will begin thinking about your own. Every person is unique. Every team and organization is also unique. Therefore, everyone will leave their own unique fingerprints. What are yours? Once you know what they are, they can become a unifying element of your team and a great filter through which you can choose who belongs on your team and who doesn't.

---

[34]Someone once said that the customer is always right. Really? I don't think so. At The Latimer Group, we approach each client interaction ready to complement and reinforce what is correct, and ready to respectfully and honestly tell the client what is not. Each client is treated with the utmost respect, but treating someone with respect does not mean always saying, "You're right." No one is always right—not even the customer. True, the customer is always entitled to respect. But part of your value to your clients should be the confidence to look them in the eye and simply say, "You're wrong."

# SHARING THE SANDBOX

chapter 7: principles of followership

*Not everything that counts can be counted.*
*And not everything counted counts.*
**– Albert Einstein**


Here's a simple fact: Our business culture is obsessed with leadership.

Each year, we spend many thousands of hours and seemingly countless dollars studying it, teaching it, observing it, and commenting on it. Take a walk down the business-publication aisle in almost any bookstore, and you'll see what I mean: book after book after book on leadership. When organizations have money to burn on professional development, leadership skills are always on the menu. Peruse any news website and you'll find enough commentary on leadership to make your head spin.

It's all for good reason. Leadership is a critical component in the success equation, whether we are talking about business, sports, or politics. But every successful equation has more than one component. Leaders need followers, and if teams require strong leadership to be successful, it follows that they also need something else—something beyond leadership.

Here's another simple fact: While we spend all this time and money teaching and learning leadership, we spend comparatively nothing teaching and learning the concept of "followership." There can be no leadership without followership, and there can be no followership without leadership. The two concepts are inextricably linked, yet we obsess over one while ignoring the other.[35] This is a problem. In fact, when someone is described as a follower, it is often used in a derogatory sense. We celebrate the leader, but we denigrate the follower. It is part of our cultural DNA.

The American business community's obsession with leadership can be attributed, in part, to what we'll call the American Myth. Scan any textbook on American history and you'll see tale after tale of the rugged individualism that we Americans have long celebrated. Every nation has its own mythology, and in America, our mythology is based on individuals who pull themselves up by their own bootstraps, make decisions, execute plans, persevere, and move forward. These heroes almost always have a sidekick of some sort, but this person rarely reaches the mythological status of the hero. Hollywood often turns the sidekick into a comic distraction or a modest voice of occasional wisdom.[36] The problem is not limited to Hollywood's storytelling; just look at how the advertising industry positions automobiles: *Lead, never follow… Drivers wanted…* the list goes on and on.

Followership skills are critical to any team's success. We all need to know how to be good teammates. We all need to know how to support others who are in the lead. Consider this: No one, and I mean *no one*, leads all the time. Some of us lead some of the time, a few of us lead a lot of the time, but none of us leads all the time. And the fundamental point in this chapter is that those who lead best also know how to follow others when the time comes.

---

[35] Key Concept #12: Think about leading and following.

[36] Examples of the mythological hero-sidekick dynamic abound: Batman and Robin; Robin Hood and any one of his "merry men"; Martin Riggs and Danny Murtaugh; Axel Foley and Rosewood and Taggart; The Godfather's Michael and Fredo; Dr. Evil and Mini Me; The Lone Ranger and Tonto; Han Solo and Chewbacca; Lucy Ricardo and Ethel Mertz; Butch and Sundance, who became mythological together, as a pair; Laverne De Fazio an Shirley Feeney, although much like Butch and Sundance, they are often viewed more as a pair; Don Quixote and Sancho Panza… the list could get incredibly long.

What makes a good follower? It's not that complicated. The concepts are simple to understand but often complicated to execute. Why? Because a little something called "the ego" gets in the way.

But if we can manage the ego; embrace the fact that there is value to ourselves, our teammates, *and* our leaders; and be good teammates and followers; then we have a chance to do something great.[37] So with all of this in mind, here are a few practices that will make you a great teammate and follower:

1. **Be part of the process.** Strong followers are not just along for the ride. They contribute to the process. Strong leaders seek the input of others in their organization, and strong followers seek to contribute whenever possible and appropriate. Even if they are disappointed to be following, strong followers don't distance themselves from the plan. They are willing to contribute an idea or a suggestion, but when the time comes to execute the plan, they focus on helping out rather than complaining that they are not in charge.

2. **Be open to ideas other than your own.** Strong followers give input and contribute, but they also realize that good ideas can come from others, too. Listen to what others have to say. Listen with your ears *and* your mind.

3. **Disagree internally, support externally.** Strong followers on good teams have a responsibility to raise their hand and speak up when they disagree with something. But strong followers always share that disagreement respectfully, logically, and *internally within the team*. Once a decision is made final, the strong follower supports it and does everything they can to make it work. Strong followers speak up and then get onboard once the decision is made.

4. **Celebrate the performances of others.** Strong followers en-

---

[37] Here's a great quote from an unlikely source: "To be a good leader, at some point you have to be a good follower. I was always a good follower. I always followed the right people and listened to the right things. Those helped shape me as a leader." Great words from NBA point guard Chauncey Billups—a guy who is known throughout the league for being a great leader.

joy and celebrate the successes of their teammates. Strong followers cheer for the people around them and love to see their teams succeed—regardless of whether the spotlight shines on them themselves. The strong follower, just like the strong leader, thinks and speaks of "we" and rarely of "I."[38]

5.  **Carry your own weight.** Being a strong cheerleader is important, but to be a valuable member of a team, you must also do the legwork. Everyone loves to have a positive cheerleader on the team, but eventually, if that cheerleader does not actively contribute to the team's success, the cheering starts to ring hollow.

6.  **Don't run for office.** Strong followers do lots of things that may eventually make them a candidate for a leadership position, but strong followers don't actively campaign to replace the current leadership. Strong followers do their job well, and they are ready when the time comes to step forward and assume a more prominent role on the team.

7.  **Keep the "dirty laundry" within the team.** This point is similar to #3, but is still worth a separate mention. Strong followers don't publicly criticize a teammate or team leadership. They keep their issues within the team. Weak teams don't.

Followership isn't always fun; it's not always sexy. The credit often goes to the person in the lead. But good followership can have its own rewards since the best teams celebrate the successes of the whole group. The best leaders share the credit with the people around them. And on the best teams, there is pride felt throughout the team, among both the leaders and the followers.[39]

---

[38]We'll cover this topic in more detail in the next chapter, but here's a quick explanation. "I" is not a bad word. But it is an exclusive word. And teams and team building are about inclusion and making people feel like they are part of something—connected to the group. When someone constantly speaks in the first-person singular ("I"), it can be highly alienating to teammates. The best communicators make the audience feel like they are part of something, part of a common cause or effort. And despite what might be going on inside your own head, if you constantly say "I," people will eventually conclude that you care mostly about yourself. Are you an "I" speaker or a "we" speaker? Have you ever recorded yourself and actually checked? It might be illuminating.

[39]QUIZ #3: How good a teammate are you? (See quizzes at the end of Part 1.)

# SHARING THE SANDBOX

*"It's a terrible thing to look over your shoulder
when you are trying to lead, and find no one there."*
**– Franklin Delano Roosevelt**

In the previous chapter, we established that because no one leads all the time, it's important to know how to act when someone else is in charge. That skill will help you make your team stronger, whether you are a follower or a leader. Most people have to follow for a while before they are given a chance to lead. All the better—our experience as a member of a team can really inform and enhance our experience as the leader of one.

Let me return to the years 1995 through 2000, when I trained for the 2000 US Olympic Sailing Team. My experiences as an Olympic aspirant were life-altering in many ways. For one thing, they gave me the chance to think about how I would lead America's Olympic sailing program if I were ever asked. I never really thought it would happen, but it did. In October 2004, I was asked to serve as Chairman of the US Olympic and Paralympic Sailing Program. Not a day goes by that I don't think back to my experiences as an athlete in the program. I constantly draw on my days as a member of the team, and I like to believe that those days have had a direct impact on my experiences as the program's leader.

Some people like to say that leaders are simply born, that most, if not all, leadership is natural. I think this is only partially true. I don't think anyone is born with a complete set of necessary tools and skills. Great leadership is a combination of some nature (some are born without any desire to lead) and some nurture (most leaders have acquired many skills along the way in addition to their natural gifts). Leadership is neither all nature nor all nurture. There is some of both in all leaders.

But how much of each? That really depends on the situation and the desire of the leader-to-be. I've seen examples on all sides of this discussion: the person with absolutely zero leadership nature who tries to be seen as a leader (and struggles mightily); the person with limited leadership nature but a strong desire to improve who, thus, becomes a strong leader; the person with plenty of leadership nature who never works to improve and eventually peaks as a mediocre leader; and the person with plenty of leadership nature who works hard at it and becomes truly great.

As we wrote earlier, some leadership nature is required. But it merits repeating that no amount of leadership nature will ever eliminate the need for some nurture, some effort to work at the skills and improve. No matter how natural a leader someone might appear to be, there will always, *always* be a need to focus on the skill, improve, and raise the leadership abilities to a higher level.

For those of you who are interested in nurturing yourself to a higher level of leadership, here are some things to think about:

1. **Set direction and goals.** Great leaders understand that they are responsible for making sure their organization has direction, a mission, and clear goals. Without these things, the organization wanders in the wilderness with no path to follow. Establishing direction and goals can—and should—be a group effort. But responsibility for the quality of this work lies squarely on the shoulders of the group leader. On a personal level, I like a collaborative model for direction and goals because collaboration

creates ownership (more on that in a moment). But don't let a desire for collaboration diminish your understanding that if you lead the team or the group or the organization, this one falls on your shoulders. Collaboration is great. But at some point, you need to take the collaborative output and put something specific and final down on paper for all to see and read.

2.  **Communicate the direction and goals broadly.** Regardless of how much collaboration you relied on in the goals-creation phase, once the goals and the direction are determined, they need to be communicated to all. Having a set of goals is a great thing, but if no one knows what they are, they serve no purpose. The goals and the direction have to be known if they are to have any value. I remember clearly meeting the president of a regional New England bank (let's call it "Wadsworth Bank"). The bank's leadership had a very clear sense of what they were trying to accomplish as an organization. In fact, they had little wallet cards printed up that included the tenets of the "Wadsworth Way." Every employee was expected to have one with them at all times and know all the elements of the Wadsworth Way. There were plenty of examples of Wadsworth's president dropping in unannounced at a local branch and asking a random teller to talk about the "Wadsworth Way." I'm sure some were intimidated by this, and some may have even dreaded the sight of him walking through the front door, but he made a point of making sure that the company's direction and goals were understood throughout the organization. It's leadership's responsibility to set goals. It's also leadership's responsibility to make sure people in the organization know what the goals and direction are.

3.  **Create ownership, roles, and responsibilities—and a plan.** Once the goals and the direction are set and understood, it's time to create some ownership. This can be done in lots of ways, including a collaborative process in the goal-setting phase. Good leaders constantly work toward creating owner-

ship, but the most critical time to do so is the plan-creation phase. Goals are critical, but at some point, you need a plan to help you reach those goals. A successful planning phase includes the steps in the plan *and* who is responsible for each of them. In other words, a good planning phase includes the creation of roles and responsibilities for everyone on the team. Human beings like to know how they are contributing to a particular outcome. They like to belong; they like to have a role, a place. Without a role within the team, without a set of responsibilities, it is hard for someone to feel a sense of ownership over the team. If you want everyone on your team to care, they need to feel connected, and the only way to accomplish this is to have specific duties.

4. **Practice what you preach.** This is an important one for the leader. This is where the leader moves beyond the use of words to lead the team and relies on actual action. Words are critical. Communication skills are a mission-critical skill for any leader. But words without consistent actions are eventually seen as hollow. Good leaders are very conscious of how they want others to act within the team, and they model those exact behaviors. If you want people to come in early, you better be in early. If you want people to dress or act a certain way, you better show them how it is done. If you want a culture of respect within your organization, then you need to show them what that respect looks like. The simple fact is that you, as the leader, set the tone and the environment for your team. People will watch you closely, more closely than when you were simply a member of the team. The scrutiny is much higher. People will parse your words, watch your actions closely. Embrace it. It is the price of admission to lead, and good teams depend on leadership that practices what it preaches.

5. **Listen when you can; make decisions when you must.** Earlier in this book, we discussed the realities of the 21st century that cannot be ignored. I feel strongly that the world we live in

mandates a different approach to leadership than might have been appropriate even 15-20 years ago. People have more information, they have more to say, and they have a greater sense of entitlement to say it. They want to speak and be heard. Leaders must embrace these realities, and listening skills are critical. The days of the autocratic leader who commands from the ivory tower with no contact from the commoners is long, long outdated. The 21st-century leader knows how to ask questions, actually listens to the answers, and embraces the fact that good ideas can come from anywhere in the organization. But, but, BUT… there also comes a time when the good leader needs to pause the information-gathering mode and move to the decision-making phase. We can't just listen forever. At some point, decisions have to be made and actions need to begin. The natural question, therefore, is, "When does the good leader move from listening to decision-making?" It really does depend on the nature of the situation, the maturity of the team, and the urgency of the matter. Good leaders never stop listening, but they know when to move from an information-gathering phase and into a planning and decision-making phase.

6. **Get to know your people well; meet them where they are.** In chapter 2, we referenced a flexible leadership style. The simple fact is that since no two people are the same, the natural extension is that no two teams can be the same either. Every team is made up of unique individuals, who each bring their own strengths, weaknesses, confidences, and insecurities to the team equation. The good leader will understand this and not look at all people as identical and replaceable parts. Obviously, the larger the organization, the harder it is to know *everyone* in the organization. But the concept applies no matter the size of the organization. While the most senior leadership in a large organization may not be able to know everyone, he or she can model this behavior with the people he or she does

interact with and set that tone for the entire organization. The acknowledgement that I am not exactly the same as the person standing next to me is a sign of respect for me and the person next to me. And the leader who shows me that respect has earned a measure of respect back from me. Furthermore, when I understand what makes you tick as a person and a professional, I am much more likely to be able to deploy your skills in the most effective way for the benefit of the team. Understanding what makes your people different builds a stronger team dynamic through demonstrated respect, and it is also more efficient. You'll get better results.

7. **Push people beyond their comfort zones.** It's important that we understand the people on our teams and that we meet them where they are developmentally, emotionally, and professionally. But just because we need to meet them where they are, does not mean we should be content to let them stay where they are. Good leaders help their people develop and grow. Good leaders push their people to take on more responsibility, to set higher goals, and to be more ambitious. Start off by trying to understand where they are when you begin working with them, but then spend time thinking about how you can help them move to a better, more productive place.

8. **Be flexible in your style and approach.** Let's take the last point a step further. If we agree that our people are unique and that, therefore, each team situation is unique, then a flexible leadership style is required. The leader who tries to apply a one-size-fits-all approach to their leadership is setting themselves and their team up for underperformance. Different scenarios call for different styles. In fact, the point that is really being made here is that good leaders have a high emotional IQ and understand how and when to adjust their approach based on the situation and the need. For example, some situations may call for very inclusive, collaborative, communicative styles of leadership. When there is time to be seeking input and

when we are trying to build a positive energy within the team, this style can be appropriate. On the other extreme, certain situations may call for more of a commanding leadership style, when there are mission critical issues and great urgency. You can apply many types of styles, but the point here is that you should first acknowledge that you will need more than one style along the way, and that the good leader will be aware of changing dynamics and the need for an adjustment in style. There is value in a leader who has perfected one specific style, but that person's overall value is narrow. Once their expertise is no longer needed, their value disappears. We are more interested in helping you become a leader who can add value across the spectrum of challenges.[40]

9.  **Share credit, motivate through acclimation.** Too many leaders make the mistake of taking credit for themselves. If your name appears at the top of the organizational chart and the team succeeds, an appropriate amount of credit will naturally come to you. Successful outcomes usually generate plenty of credit to go around for everyone, so share it broadly. Rather than spend energy talking credit for yourself, spend your energy spreading it around to others. Be inclusive. Make the people on the team feel good about the success. Make sure they know they are appreciated. Give them some time to shine in the spotlight.

    When you give credit to others, it will build their affinity toward the team and toward you, both very good things if you care about building good teams. If you take the credit for yourself, no one will be excited to follow you. Even if they wanted to pat you on the back, they can't because you own hand is already there!

---

[40]For those who are interested, I highly recommend any of the books by Daniel Goleman, who writes on the topic of emotional intelligence as well as anyone I have read.

Sometimes the smallest words speak the loudest. And some-times the most common words can provide the deepest in-sight into how we really feel. Let me ask you a question. Are you an "I" leader or are you a "we" leader? Are you sure? Have you ever recorded yourself while speaking and actually count-ed how often you say "I" as opposed to "we"? It can be quite telling, and I encourage you to try it. "We" is an inclusive word. It describes the group as a whole and shares credit broadly. "I" is an exclusive, solitary word. Your choice of pronoun can have a significant impact on how you are perceived by those around you.

Here's a case in point, from the 2008 US presidential election. During the Democratic Party primaries, Barack Obama and Hilary Clinton were locked in a close fight for the presidential nomination. On January 3, 2008, Barack Obama won the Iowa caucus, the first major test in the 2008 presidential primary season. Five days later, on January 8, Hilary Clinton won the New Hampshire primary. In each case, the winning candidate gave the customary victory speech to a roomful of rabid sup-porters. In each case, the victor spoke for about 15 minutes. (Each speech is still easily found on www.youtube.com.)

Here is the opening passage from candidate Obama's speech:

> *They said this day would never come. They said our sights were set too high. They said this country was too divided, too disillusioned, to ever come together around a common purpose. But on this January night, at this defining moment in history, you have done what the cynics said we could not do. You have done what the state of New Hampshire can do in five days. You have done what America can do in this new year, 2008. In lines that stretched around schools and churches, in small towns and in big cities, you came together as Democrats, Republicans, and Independents, to stand up and say that we are one nation, that we are one people, and*

*that our time for change has come.*

And here is the opening passage from candidate Clinton's speech:

> *I come tonight with a very full heart, and I want especially to thank New Hampshire. Over the last week, I listened to you, and in the process, I found my own voice. I felt like we all spoke from our hearts, and I am so gratified that you responded. Now, together, let's give America the kind of comeback that New Hampshire has just given me.*

The contrast is startling. Obama's message is one of unity and inclusion, with not a single "I" in the first few sentences. In fact, throughout that campaign, Obama almost never used the first-person singular. His message throughout that campaign was rarely about him, and almost always about the people he was speaking to.

Clinton's message, on the other hand, left a very different impression. Whether she intended to or not, she left the impression that she cared mostly about herself. Her dominant pronoun choice throughout that entire speech was "I." This was a common critique of her speaking style throughout that campaign; it was not just an isolated incident.

What can we draw from this? Rest assured, I'm not making any political judgment or endorsement of any kind. I'm merely commenting on the choice of language and how the smallest pronouns can leave large impressions.

10. **Treat everyone with respect.** I think this point is already built into so many of the other points in this chapter. But it is worth mentioning directly and independently. Teams are built on many things, but respect is near the top of the list. Great teams consist of people who may not be the best of friends all the time, but when in the team environment, they treat each other with the highest level of professional respect. This kind of re-

spect can come in many forms: giving clear roles and responsibilities; saying hello and taking an interest in people; saying,
"Nice job" when appropriate; including people in conversations they should be included in; not always expecting them
to modify their style to yours, but rather showing that you also
can modify your style to theirs; respecting confidences; avoiding judgment. This could quickly become a very long list. But
the point here is that great teams are built on respect, and respect starts with the team's leadership.

Great leadership is not about a list of specific steps to be memo-
rized. We can't apply the same things in the same sequence every time.
As we have pointed out previously in these pages, every team situation
is different, and any attempt to apply the same exact approach or set
of steps over and over will almost certainly cause your team and your
leadership experience to fall short of expectation. Good leadership is
not a rigid road map of "First do this, go one mile, turn left, then do this
..." It just doesn't work that way. Great leadership is about having a set
of firm principles that can be applied broadly over time.[41]

---

[41]QUIZ #4: How good a leader are you? (See quizzes at the end of Part 1.)

# SHARING THE SANDBOX

chapter 9: summary of
key concepts in part 1

*In life, in real life, we aren't pitted against one another; we are pitted against*
*ourselves, and our victories are almost always ones we forge alone.*

– **Richard Bode, from First You Have to Row a Little Boat**

In Part 1 of *Sharing the Sandbox*, we examined some of fundamental principles of teams, team building, leadership, and followership. Here are the key concepts for you to take away:

1.  **Create alignment.** This is the key goal when building a team, and the central idea in this book. When you lead, try to align followers around the idea, the goal, the plan, or the ethos of the team; aim to create a group of people moving forward as one. When you succeed in doing this, your team will be able to devote all of its competitive energy outwardly, at the goal or the competition, without wasting any of it on internal issues. Alignment is the ultimate goal in building a team.

2.  **Create ownership.** Great teams consist of people who care enough about the outcome to "own" it. You will want the people on your team to take a vested interest in the outcome, to do more than just punch the clock and collect a paycheck. You want people who care deeply about a successful outcome and

help to achieve it.

3. **Be flexible.** Each person is unique, and so it follows that each team will be unique. This is a key concept in the 21st century, because as people become more informed, more connected, and more opinionated, each group situation becomes more complicated. The more informed and opinionated your colleagues are, the harder it becomes to get them aligned around *anything*. This means you'll need to take a flexible approach to each situation. Just because something worked for you in the past does not mean it will work again in the future.

4. **Open the lines of communication.** Great teams require open and functional communication; open and functional communication allows for the possibility of alignment. Team members cannot align without honest communication around the goals, the plan, and how to execute the plan. Only when we can openly discuss and debate the issues, do we have the opportunity to create alignment.

5. **Practice what you preach.** Great teams consist of people who behave the way they expect others to. This refers not just to the leadership, although this is absolutely required of good leaders, but is also a requirement for everyone else on the team. When each member of your team demonstrates the behaviors expected from others, and when each member of the team holds himself or herself to the same standard he or she applies to others, we will have created a dynamic of positive reinforcement and respect.

6. **Balance goals with tasks.** Goals are critical. But a goal without a plan is just a wish. Once you have settled on your goals, shift your focus and efforts to creating specific tasks that will help you reach them.

7. **Control the controllable.** There are things within our control and things that are beyond our control. Focus on controlling the aspects of the team's performance that are controllable.

Once you have done this, you can shift your focus to other variables.

8.  **Plan for the uncontrollable.** It's not enough to say, "That's beyond my control, so I won't worry about it." Successful teams, while they might not obsess about the uncontrollable, will still consider what *might happen* and create plans and decision-making frameworks so that when something unexpected or uncontrollable happens, they are prepared to react. Great teams might even play out possible scenarios ahead of time. ("If this happens, we'll do X . . . If that happens we'll do Y.")

9.  **Be memorable.** Great teams are fueled by great communication, and great communication is based, in part, on the speaker's ability to make the key points memorable. If the audience (or, in this case, the team) has to work too hard to parse the speaker's (leader's) words, most will eventually stop trying. A great goal during preparation, therefore, is to make sure people will remember what you say. Make it easy for the audience to connect and recall the key elements of your message.

10. **Collaborate.** Great teams are based on not only the ability to collaborate, but also a desire to do so. Followers and leaders alike need to be committed to working with others and pooling their talents to produce greater performance than they would on their own.

11. **Encourage authenticity.** Authenticity is about trusting each other with our authentic selves, and it's about accepting each other for what we are. Great teams give people the freedom to be who and what they are. Great teams do *not* cause people to waste energy worrying about how they should act. Great leaders encourage team members to focus their energy on the task at hand rather than on hiding some aspect of themselves.

12. **Think about leading *and* following.** Great teams need more than just great leaders. They need great people throughout the team from the top to the bottom. They need people who

know how to lead and how to follow—and are comfortable in both roles.

Great teams create their own success, and they start with people who want to work well with others, who *want* to share the sandbox in a positive and effective way.[42] These concepts are fundamental to building great teams. If we didn't look first at the foundations of successful teams, as we have done in Part 1 of this book, then there would be no point in moving on to steps of team building found in Part 2. Great teams start with people who have the proper attitude about themselves and the people around them. When we have the correct mindset, then—and only then—can we discuss the steps it takes to build great teams.

---

[42] Andrew Carnegie: "Take away everything else but leave me my organization and in 10 years I'll be back on top." His point was clear. In his mind, the things that got him to the top were his team and his organization. And if you took away all the other market and financial advantages he enjoyed, he believed he could return to the top if he had the right people around him.

# Part 1 Quizzes: Test Yourself

**Quiz #1: Is your leadership style collaborative or authoritarian?**
For each of the following questions, write the number corresponding to the answer that fits best.

1—Always    2—Frequently    3—Occasionally    4—Never

1.  How often do you ask team members, "What do you think?"  \_\_\_\_\_
2.  How often do you implement proposals that come from team members?  \_\_\_\_\_
3.  How often do team members voice dissent?  \_\_\_\_\_
4.  When team members voice dissent, how often do you take it into consideration?  \_\_\_\_\_
5.  How often do you analyze team members' strengths and weaknesses?  \_\_\_\_\_
6.  How often do you ask your team members to evaluate progress?  \_\_\_\_\_
7.  How often do you ask your team members to give feedback on the team?  \_\_\_\_\_
8.  How often do people say to you, "I would love to work with you some time"?  \_\_\_\_\_
9.  How often do you think of ways to give each team member a stake in the outcome?  \_\_\_\_\_
10. How often do you ask your team members for feedback on you?  \_\_\_\_\_

**Total Score**  \_\_\_\_\_

**Rate your score:**
10-15: Highly collaborative
16-24: Somewhat collaborative
25-32: Somewhat authoritarian
33-40: Very authoritarian

If you really want to test yourself, ask team members to take the same quiz and rate you. Compare the answers. How did your own perception compare to the perceptions of others?

### Quiz #2: How well do you prepare to communicate?

For each of the following questions, write the number corresponding to the answer that fits best.

1—Always    2—Frequently    3—Occasionally    4—Never

1. Prior to speaking, how often do you think about your goals? ____
2. Prior to speaking, how often do you think about who will be listening? ____
3. Prior to speaking, how often do you think about what matters most to the audience? ____
4. Prior to speaking, how often do you try to anticipate likely audience objections? ____
5. How often do you present your audience with key next steps? ____
6. How often does your audience ask you questions you fully anticipated? ____
7. How often do you get the outcome you planned for prior to your communication? ____
8. How often do you think you have thoroughly planned out your communication? ____
9. How often do you actually practice your message/speech/presentation out loud? ____
10. How often do you debrief your performance in anticipation of the next opportunity? ____

**Total Score** ____

**Rate your score:**
10-15: Great planner
16-24: Good planner
25-32: Mediocre planner
33-40: Poor planner

If you really want to test yourself, ask team members to take the same quiz and rate you. Compare the answers. How did your own perception compare to the perceptions of others?

## Quiz #3: How good a teammate are you?

For each of the following questions, write the number corresponding to the answer that fits best.

1—Always    2—Frequently    3—Occasionally    4—Never

1. Do you work hard to contribute to the outcome?          _____
2. Do you listen to ideas/input from others?               _____
3. Do you promote the successes of others on the team?     _____
4. Do you worry about getting your own
   job done before you try to help others?                 _____
5. Do you support the leadership of the team?              _____
6. Do you keep your criticism internal to the team?        _____
7. Do you support the direction of the team externally?    _____
                                       **Total Score**     _____

### Rate your score:

7-10: Great Teammate

11-15: Good Teammate

16-20: Mediocre Teammate

21-28: Poor Teammate

If you really want to test yourself, ask team members to take the same quiz and rate you. Compare the answers. How did your own perception compare to the perceptions of others?

## Quiz #4: How good a leader are you?

For each of the following questions, write the number corresponding to the answer that fits best.

1—Always    2—Frequently    3—Occasionally    4—Never

1.  I plan out the team's goals. _____
2.  I make sure everyone understands what the goals are. _____
3.  I make sure everyone knows their role and responsibilities. _____
4.  I listen to the opinions of others and seek input. _____
5.  I try to practice what I preach. _____
6.  I communicate with the team regularly. _____
7.  I try to understand each person on the team and what I can do to help each perform. _____
8.  I share credit publicly. _____
9.  I encourage people to be ambitious and try to push them past their comfort zone. _____
10. I encourage a culture of mutual respect within the team. _____

**Total Score** _____

### Rate your score:
10-15: Strong Leader
16-24: Good Leader
25-32: Mediocre Leader
33-40: Poor Leader

If you really want to test yourself, ask team members to take the same quiz and rate you. Compare the answers. How did your own perception compare to the perceptions of others?

# PART 2

## Tools and Frameworks

THE LATIMER GROUP

# SHARING THE SANDBOX

## chapter 10: in pursuit of alignment—introducing ARROW

*Coming together is a beginning. Keeping together is progress.*
*Working together is success.*

**– Henry Ford**

Alignment: that's our goal.

We want to create teams that have concrete goals and a plan to achieve those goals. We want to create teams with people who are all marching in the same direction, following the same plan toward the same result. We want to create teams that are focused outwardly at the competition and at the challenge at hand, not inwardly at each other.[43] We want nothing less than *great* team experiences.

But how do we accomplish this? How do we encourage the people around us to work together toward a common goal in a functional and productive way? It sounds hard to do. And in many ways, it is. But it's not impossible, and with the proper frameworks and approaches, combined with the right attitude, alignment is achievable.

---

[43] If you are still taking notes, we'll continue highlighting the key concepts in Part 2. This is Key Concept #1 from Part 2: Recognize alignment. How do we know when our team is aligned? We know our team is aligned when all the energy on the team is focused outwardly at the competition or the issue at hand. If we are spending time and energy focused inwardly, we almost certainly have alignment problems.

If we can learn how to create alignment consistently, we'll have one of the most powerful tools in our toolbox. We don't want occasional or accidental success. We want repeatable outcomes and a greater chance of success. That's where ARROW comes in.

ARROW is the acronym for the most important elements of team alignment and the resultant team success. When we take a challenging concept such as alignment and break it down into its component parts, it becomes much more possible to achieve consistent success.

The elements of ARROW are these:

**A**lignment = (Clear **R**oles and Responsibilities) + (**R**espect for the Team and Each Other) + (**O**wnership of the Outcome) + (**W**illingness to Work)

As you know from reading the first part of this book, clear goals are step one. Once you have established clear goals, ARROW can provide the framework you need to build **A**lignment around those goals.

With Alignment as our goal, let's examine the other components of ARROW more closely.

## Clear Roles and Responsibilities

Clarity on roles and responsibilities is critical. Without it, team members may waste time on duplicated effort and leave other areas of the project untended. Without clarity here, team members may step on each other's toes, which usually creates tension. As the size of the team grows, so does the potential for duplicated effort—and the need for clear roles and responsibilities.

I've seen all sorts of examples on this topic. I've witnessed the scenario where lack of role clarity led to large gaps between the understood responsibilities on the team. It wasn't clear where one person's role ended and the next person's began, and there were big gaps between them. Important things fell through those gaps and just didn't get done. And I've also witnessed the opposite, where lack of role clarity led to duplication of effort and wasted time. In either case, lack of role clarity almost always leads to sub-optimal productivity, and also to hard feelings on the team.

So what, specifically, does role clarity mean? It means that the team members on an aligned team understand how everyone fits into the big picture. An aligned team has clear job descriptions and clear responsibilities for everyone involved. Everyone knows not only what they are doing, but also what everyone else is doing, so that all are productively contributing to a successful outcome. Everyone on the team understands the strengths and weaknesses of everyone else and knows why each member of the team is on the team. An aligned team has a clearly defined and understood organizational structure, and that structure is sacred.

Imagine your team members as pieces of a puzzle. On an aligned team, everyone understands how they all fit together as part of the big picture. Here is how you can make that happen:

1. Clarity on roles and responsibilities begins with the first steps we take when we build our team, which we will discuss in more detail in chapter 11.

2. Clarity truly starts with simply mapping the tasks and skills needed to reach the project goal, and then making sure all the necessary tasks and skills are covered by various members of the team.

3. Clarity requires that there is not too much overlap among team members. All team members need to understand what their part of the sandbox is, and where everyone else's part is as well.

4. Clarity also requires that everyone on the team has *enough to do*. When you have underutilized team members, their natural capacity and ambition to do more will cause them to seek more responsibilities and more tasks, and a typically performance-oriented person (the type we all want on our teams) will drift into other parts of the sandbox.

5. Finally, role clarity is never "done." It requires maintenance and occasional checks to ensure that everyone's understanding on roles remains clear. In meetings, I'll often ask, "Is anyone see-

ing anything that is not getting done?" I'll ask that publicly, probing for gaps in our team. I'll also ask something like, "Are you bumping into anyone on the team? Do we have too much overlap?" (These sorts of questions are best asked privately, so as not to pit one teammate against another in a public forum.)

The hardest part of role clarity is in the details, in the gray areas between the responsibilities of team members. In most cases, the macro aspects of a job description are easy enough to describe and understand. But where does one person's job description end and the next person's begin? It's not always clear, and this is where the ambition of your team members can actually cause trouble. Goal-oriented, performance-oriented people almost always seek additional responsibilities. And the easiest place to seek additional responsibilities is in the areas adjacent to the current job description. The risk is highest when a stronger personality starts to roll over someone who is capable but perhaps not as opportunistic.

You may not solve all the gray-area questions on role clarity right at the outset of our team-building effort, and that's OK. But you'll need to be conscious of them because that's where the tension almost always percolates. This will need regular attention throughout the life of the team.

Clarity on roles and responsibilities is not the most difficult thing to accomplish—but it is one of the most important.[44]

## Respect for the Team as a Whole and as Individuals

An aligned team has respect—and lots of it. An aligned team respects members' roles and responsibilities. An aligned team respects confidences. An aligned team respects the process of decision making. The members of an aligned team don't have to be the best of friends,

---

[44] Key Concept #2: Clarity on roles and responsibilities is essential.

but they do have to be supportive of each other within the context of the team and its mission.[45]

How can you tell if your team is respectful? If there is a problem between teammates on an aligned, respectful team, the problem is dealt with internally in an honest way. And once the problem is dealt with, everyone moves on without turning the disagreement into a public spectacle. Members of an aligned team respect everyone's time by showing up to meetings on time and prepared, by meeting deadlines, by delivering what they promise to deliver. Members of an aligned, respectful team respect confidences, respect others' areas of responsibility, seek input from teammates when appropriate and ask questions, listen to answers, and don't gossip or spread rumors. There are lots of examples of how a respectful team acts, and you could add to this list just as easily as I can.

The creation of a culture of respect within your team can happen in a variety of ways. It can start when you begin to choose those who will participate. Look for potential team members who are likely to be part of a respectful dynamic, people who have a natural tendency to respect others. How can you tell? I like to look for people who say thank you or who are interested in hearing how others are doing, not just telling you how they are doing. I try to avoid people who gossip or always seem to be complaining or wanting to talk about their teammates. I look for people who seem to care about others.

You can also, as the leader of a team, set a tone of respect through your own actions and behaviors. And you can create a respectful culture by consciously and openly making it a team norm, an expectation, and an open topic for discussion.

A culture of respect requires communication because perspectives differ on what is respectful and what is not. A behavior that one person thinks is acceptable may be unacceptable to another. You and I may agree that we want to be part of a respectful team culture, but we may

---

[45] We'll discuss this topic in much more detail in chapter 17, "Hard Questions with No Easy Answers."

disagree vehemently on what *that actually means*. Often in a team context, one person's "respectful" is another person's "rude."[46]

A culture of respect requires constant maintenance. Having a culture of respect is not a box that you check and then move on to something else. A culture of respect requires regular vigilance. New issues come up, new behaviors need to be examined, and perceptions of what is respectful and what is not change over time.

Without a culture of respect, you may still achieve a sense of alignment within your team. But that sense won't be authentic, and it won't last long.

## Ownership of the Outcome

An aligned team does more than just show up for work. The members of an aligned team care about the outcome of their effort and care about doing whatever they can to contribute to it. The members of an aligned team do more than just take orders and stand around waiting to be told what to do. They contribute to planning and want to add value. To quote Warren Buffett once again, "No one washes a rental car. Nothing motivates a human being like honest-to-god ownership." The members of an aligned team are not just "renting" their presence on the team. They care about the outcome, as if it were their own possession.

The question I get asked most often in our team-building and team-leadership coaching is this: How do I get my team to "own" the process and the outcome? It's not easy, for sure, but like every other component of ARROW, it gets easier if we seek out certain behaviors when choosing the people we put on our team. If we seek out team

---

[46]Key Concept #3: Respect is required and takes constant maintenance, but regular communication on this topic is also required because perspectives on what is respectful and what is not will usually differ. This is a common problem on teams. Someone does something that he or she thinks is very respectful, and it is taken in another disrespectful way by someone else. We've all seen this happen. For instance, I might know you are grieving a loss and decide to give you some space. I'm trying to respect your privacy, but you might take that distance as a sign that I don't care or that I am disrespecting your grief. Or, in the workplace, I might try to show you respect by deferring to you or being formal with you. But you might take my behaviors in a different way; perhaps you think I don't want to be close to you and don't want to get to know you. There are countless examples. The point here is that good teams will discuss and understand how each person defines "respectful" and "disrespectful."

members who are likely invest in, care about, and own the things they are a part of, we have a much greater chance of success in this area.[47]

But beyond that, how do we continue to foster ownership during the team-building process and throughout the life of the team? I think the answer is simply this: Give people a seat at the table. Give them a voice. Ask their opinion. Four of the most empowering words we can ask a colleague or a team member are "What do you think?" When we ask people what they think and give them a say in the outcome, they begin contributing to the plan; once they contribute, they feel like they now own at least a small piece of the pie. Conversely, when people are told what to do, it's as if they are just "renting" their spot on the team. But when those people are asked for an opinion, and they give one that contributes to the final plan, they are no longer renting. They are owners now.

The point here is that if we build an inclusive atmosphere where communication and input are valued, people are more likely to want to be a part of it. It's a simple fact that people have an innate desire to be listened to. Very few people come to work hoping and praying to be told what to do all day long. People want their voices to be heard. And when they are heard, they feel included, they feel better about what they are a part of, and they are much more likely to care about the success of the team.

Can people care too much? They absolutely can. And team leaders need to keep an eye out for the team member whose sense of ownership has gone beyond the productive and is approaching the destructive.[48] But if forced to choose between working with people who care too little or who care too much, I'll take "too much" every time. "Too

---

[47]When I am building a team, I like to look for people who are interested in more than the simple aspects of their job. I look for people who show an interest in the outcome, want to hear how it all fits together, and get excited about the possibilities. When I am interviewing a candidate, if their questions are all something like "How much vacation do I get?" that is red flag. But if their questions are more like "What is the team trying to achieve and how do I fit into that?" I get more interested.

[48]Keep an eye out for the person who gets easily frustrated with the team, and who explains that frustration by pointing out how much they care. It's easy for this to happen; even people with the best intentions sometimes step over the line in this way. But you need to manage this tendency closely. If a team member cares too much and starts to express frustration, it can cause others on the team to react negatively or back away from potential conflict.

much" can often be managed down a little bit.[49] "Not enough" can be coached, but often it is indicative of something deeper: an otherwise good, talented person who is in the wrong spot on the team or in the organization; perhaps a bad work ethic; perhaps something distracting from somewhere else in life.

We don't want people just showing up for work. We want people who care, who want to be there, and who protect the team and the project as if it were their own prized possession.[50]

## Willingness to Work

Finally, on an aligned team, the members of the team are all willing to roll up their sleeves and actually do the hard work to get a positive outcome. It is one thing to understand roles, be respectful, act like you own the outcome, and even be a positive, supportive teammate who cheers for others. On an aligned team, there is also agreement, formally or informally, on the level of commitment to doing the actual work. On an aligned team, everyone *actively contributes* to the bottom line. A teammate can do all the other things required in ARROW. And that teammate can openly take joy in the success of others. But that cheer-leading will eventually ring hollow if he or she does not match that by also tangibly contributing to the bottom line and by taking a fair share of the workload.[51]

---

[49] I always feel like the person who cares too much can be managed more easily than the person who cares not at all. It's hard to make someone engage on something. If he or she doesn't care, I find it really hard to make him or her care. Perhaps you can tie the outcome of the team to something beneficial to that person. But that is usually easier if your team is part of a cause or a charitable venture. People will get involved there because they care. It might be harder in the workplace because for some people work is about nothing more than the paycheck. If I have someone on my team who cares too much, I find it easier to help the person see how his or her behavior is actually hurting the chances of the outcome they want so badly.

[50] Key Concept #4: Everyone needs to own the outcome. If the people on your team are simply "renting" their spot on the team, dysfunction and/or underperformance are probably not far off. We want people to care enough to "own" it. This was also a key concept in Part 1. It merits a second mention.

[51] I've been on teams many times with people who make a great first impression. They are positive, they care about you, they cheer for others, they smile, they seem to enjoy being there, but they just don't sell enough, or do their job well enough, or contribute to the outcome or bottom line. Eventually, you realize that beyond the smile and the cheering, there just isn't that much talent or effectiveness there. This person ultimately becomes a distraction or destructive to the team. The person's lack of productivity eventually outweighs his or her positive demeanor.

"Willingness to work" is the component of ARROW that is the simplest and easiest to grasp. As team leaders and team members, we need to carry our fair share of the workload and seek out teammates who will do the same. We need to make sure that the burden of performance and workload does not fall disproportionately on any subset of the team. Everyone needs to contribute. Does everyone need to contribute an equal amount all the time? Of course not. But everyone needs to contribute consistently and substantially. Managing that delicate balance is part of the challenge of leadership, but good team leaders will have a keen sense of when the workload is getting out of balance and when a member or members of the team are no longer doing their fair share. Grossly disproportionate workloads will quickly become divisive and toxic within the team.[52]

For leaders, it is also important to show the team that you are not afraid to roll up your sleeves and do some of the undesirable work yourself. It can be highly unmotivating to work for someone who always seems to disappear when the hard labor is about to start. Team leaders need to set the tone and lean into the heavy loads. When the team leader is seen doing the most undesirable work, everyone else on the team will have a hard time avoiding that work themselves. When the tone starts at the top, it has an important trickle-down effect on the rest of the team.[53]

[52] Key Concept #5: Everyone has to substantively contribute to the bottom line. Disproportionate workloads and/ or responsibilities will eventually become a divisive factor in your team.

[53] Here's a personal example from our 2012 US Olympic Sailing Team. Our team had a training facility at the Olympic site in Weymouth, England, with meeting space, a workout area, storage, and a bathroom. In the summer of 2011, there started to be complaints that the place was getting dirty and people were not cleaning up after themselves. We made several public requests for the place to be kept neater, but nothing happened. So I started cleaning up every morning, right around the time when I knew people would be coming in. I would clean up the bathroom a bit and sweep the floor. When people saw the chairman cleaning, it had an immediate impact. Others started doing the same, and almost immediately, the place was cleaner. It was one thing for the chairman to say, "Please clean up." It was another for the chairman to actually clean up. People followed the lead more quickly than they followed the order. And an important part of this was that I cleaned in full view of everyone—not because I wanted credit for cleaning, but because I believed that seeing me clean would cause others to do the same and would create a trickle-down effect that would benefit everyone. I've made more than my fair share of leadership mistakes, but this one worked as planned.

# The Value of ARROW

There are no magic potions or pills when it comes to leading people. Building and leading teams requires a keen awareness of many things and constant vigilance. But while we discuss throughout this book the importance of things like goals, planning, and other key principles of leadership and team building, the most challenging aspect is, without question, the question of alignment. The ability to cause the people around you to join together and work toward a common goal is the key to the castle in modern team building. The 21st-century realities discussed in chapter 3 of this book make the issue of alignment harder than ever. The people around you have opinions. They want to be heard. And many of them think they can lead better than you can. Building alignment in that environment is not easy.

ARROW will help you in two primary ways:

1.  It will help you identify important characteristics, behaviors, and attitudes to look for in the people you put on your team.

2.  It will give you a simple, repeatable, quickly actionable framework with which to create the team dynamic you want (and help you maintain that dynamic on a continual basis).

If you want to be a part of successful teams, then you need to worry about alignment. And if you seek alignment, then the four components of the ARROW equation need to be at the forefront of your thinking and planning.[54]

---

[54]QUIZ #5: How well aligned is your team? (See quizzes at the end of Part 2.)

# SHARING THE SANDBOX

chapter 11: how to build a great team from the ground up

*You are looking for players who care more about the name on the front of the jersey than the name on the back.*

*– Herb Brooks*

Sometimes we lead, or become a part of, a legacy team. But other times we have the opportunity and the good fortune to build or be a member of a team from the beginning. Being able to build a team from the ground up is a gift. The clean canvas of building a brand-new team is the opportunity to do things the correct way, the way we want them done. Whether you lead the team or are tapped to become a member of it, being present for the team's genesis gives you the opportunity to create something special.

When we inherit or join an existing team, often the best way to help that team succeed is to fine-tune the parts that need work, rather than start over. (We usually don't have the time to do the latter.) Typically, when we join a team when the project or the mission has already started, we have to do what we can to keep moving forward as best and as quickly as possible. In other words, sometimes we just have to play the hand of cards we've been dealt and do the best we can.

When we can build a new team, however, we have the time for strategy to be laid, choices to be made, and planning to be done. This is potentially both a blessing and a curse. It becomes a blessing if we do a good job, and the glow of that team's success shines brightly on us. However, when we are building a team from the ground up, we own that team in all ways, and we have responsibility for that team's success or failure. This can become a curse. If we plan poorly or somehow do a bad job leading the team, it is ours, we own it, and the failure reflects badly on those who constructed the team. The initial planning needs to be taken seriously.

So, how do we plan for our new team? Here are some critical steps you can take each time you begin building a new team:

1. **Define your goals.** You've heard this before, and you'll keep hearing it. This must be your first step every single time. Decide where you are going. Decide the problem you are trying to solve or the opportunity you are trying to leverage. Decide what the purpose or mission is. This is required and critical, because only when you clearly know what goals you are trying to achieve do you have a reasonable chance of reaching them.

   Ask yourself: Are we launching a new product? Are we managing a time-sensitive project? How will we determine if we have been successful? What do we want to achieve? We must start here; this decision will shape nearly everything else that's done in the team-building process. Should your goals be focused on sales numbers, market penetration, or brand awareness? Should your goals be based on time? Will you need to get X, Y, and Z done by a certain date on the calendar? Goals come in lots of different forms. And while I cannot script them for you here, I can tell you that without them, your team is dead on arrival, before you even take your first step.

2. **Identify the necessary skills before you start choosing names.** Once you know where you want the team to go, you need to profile the skill sets that individual members need to possess to achieve the goals. Will your success be determined

by your ability to manage cost, hit timelines, expand creativity, or something else entirely? What skills will you need to achieve your goals? What technical expertise will you need? Will you need someone with certain relationships, judgment, or experience?

You should notice here that we are not yet talking about naming candidates. Discussing names of potential team members too early in the process can be dangerous and counterproductive. Doing so can lead to conscious or subconscious decisions on whom we want before we are sure that person is the correct fit. You can have an incredibly talented individual with a great attitude who might not be a good fit on your team. This second step is not about names. It is about focusing on the skills you'll need to accomplish your goals. As a starting point, complete the following sentence: "If we are going to reach our goals, we will really need a person or people who can _____."

What I'm recommending here is that you practice *keeping the emotion out of your decision making*. When we begin our search by immediately examining names, we introduce an element of emotion into the decision making. This can lead to basing our decisions on whether we like someone (or not), or get along with them (or not), or for some reason want them around (or not).

Rather, consistent and successful team assembly should include a strong element of skill-based analysis first. Later in the process, we can examine if the personalities will mesh. But successful teams start with the necessary skills and abilities. Later on, we can nurture a collaborative environment where people will get along. On the other hand, we cannot later on create technical expertise or magically conjure someone with the necessary relationships. Great team building starts with having the appropriate skills and talents.

3.  **Identify the necessary behaviors (no names yet, please).**
    So now you know where you are going and the skills you will
    need to get there, but we're still not ready to discuss names.
    When building a new team from scratch, you also need to pro-
    file the correct behaviors. By that I mean that you should make
    a conscious choice about the ways you want the people on
    your team to behave. Is your team cross-functional and does it
    include people from lots of different parts of a large organiza-
    tion? If so, you probably want people who communicate well
    and are willing to reach outside of their silo. Is your team glob-
    al, with lots of different cultures and native languages present?
    If so, you probably want people who have a global mindset
    and innately understand that not everyone acts, speaks, and
    thinks exactly like they do.

    That "perfect" candidate with the right skills that we described
    in the preceding paragraph might also be difficult to work
    with, or a terrible communicator, or slow on meeting dead-
    lines. Once you decide those behaviors are important to your
    success, then that perfect candidate with the correct skills may
    turn out to be not so perfect after all. So, in addition to profil-
    ing the skills you'll need, you should also profile the *behaviors*
    that will be conducive to a positive team dynamic.

    There is a strong element of judgment here. We cannot always
    predict whether that cocktail of personalities will work. Even
    the best judges of talent and students of people won't pre-
    dict correctly all of the time. We make our best judgments and
    know that we won't always get it right. But if we get it right
    more often than not, we're doing pretty well.

4.  **Identify the rules and expectations (still no names!).** Now
    that you know where you want to go and what skills and be-
    haviors you want potential team members to possess, it's time
    to start setting some ground rules for your team. A framework
    of team norms will foster agreement on how you will treat

each other, work together, communicate, plan, meet, and so forth. How do you expect people to behave? What do you expect them to always do? What do you expect them to never do?

This step has two major benefits. First, such a framework can be used to screen potential team members. You can present these rules and expectations and ask them, "Are you willing to be a part of this?" And second, once your team is formed and is moving forward, you can return to these pre-established rules and expectations to resolve any issues or disagreements that arise. Instead of relying on the typical emotional responses when people disagree, you can calmly go back to the rules and expectations you set out at the beginning and use those to resolve the dispute. You might even go so far as to "game out" certain potential disagreements in advance and anticipate how you would deal with them as a team. Later, if such a disagreement actually happens, you have the benefit of having already discussed, as a team, the manner in which it will be handled. Such a strategy allows you to be an objective, unemotional leader.

5.  **Start naming names.** Finally, we get to the names. Now, with goals, skills, behaviors, rules, and expectations defined, it's time to name the people who will fit with your team. Following steps one through four should allow your search to be logical and focused, since you will know what you're looking for. As I wrote earlier, I'm always intrigued by how often that "perfect" candidate everyone wanted to talk about at the beginning turns out to be not so perfect at this stage in the game—and how often the team ends up considering someone it never would have considered before.

    Once the emotion has been removed and replaced with logic, the team is much more likely to end up with candidates that fit the need, not just candidates that everyone likes. That's important, because team building is not just about assembling people we get along with. I've been on teams that got along famously but utterly failed to be productive.[55]

Although we'll return to this topic later, it bears mentioning here that great teams are not constructed of people who are great friends. Great teams are made up of people who complement each other in many ways and who can respectfully work together to achieve the goals. If the members of the team go their separate ways at the end of the day, that's OK. Some would even say it's a sign of a good team. (We'll come back to this topic later.)

6. **Create agreement on the team plan.** Once you have named your team, the last step is to bring everyone together and communicate the steps you took to build the team and why. We believe it is important for people on the team to understand the goals, skills, and behaviors that were profiled ahead of time and what the team rules and expectations are. In other words, you want people to understand why they are there and why you thought they would perform well in this particular team setting. You want people to understand how you expect them to behave individually and as a group.

Now, depending on the situation, this last step (or any of the steps, for that matter) can be done in collaboration with other key members of your team. Perhaps you are not forming the new team on your own. Perhaps you have a partner or two. Perhaps a key team member joined you from the outset and could be part of this planning. All of this does not need to be done in a vacuum. Seeking input from others can always be valuable.

---

[55] One of the telltale signs of a team that gets along well but doesn't actually produce much is that the team will spend a lot of time talking about how well everyone gets along. Why? Because very little positive outcome is actually produced, so the only positive topic of conversation is how well everyone gets along. If team harmony is a popular subject on your team, take a hard look at how well the team is actually producing.

Aim to follow a process that is logical and methodical, with decisions about team members based on what the team needs to succeed rather than whether you enjoy working with a particular person. Using these six steps can help you assemble a good, functional team in a logical way. Conversely, when we just start putting people together without forethought, we may end up with a team that is functional in one way but dysfunctional in another.

As we discussed earlier in *Sharing the Sandbox*, a team is nothing more than a collection of individuals, and since each individual is unique, then each team, by definition, is also unique. Therefore, assembling our teams in the workplace, or anywhere else, requires thought and care.[56] If we are given the luxury of building a team from the ground up, we should not waste the opportunity. Take the time to implement some thoughtful, logical steps to build that team in the correct way. You, and everyone else on your new team, will be the better for it.

---

[56]Key Concept #6: No two teams are the same. Therefore, every team is different. Each team situation needs to be considered carefully and thoughtfully.

# SHARING THE SANDBOX

chapter 12: leading the
team you inherit

*No one can whistle a symphony. It takes an orchestra to play it.*
– H. E. Luccock

Sometimes we have the luxury of building a team from the beginning. When that happens, we can take the steps, and the time, to construct the team the way we'd like. In most cases, however, we are asked to step in and lead an existing team with team members already in place, track records built, strengths and weaknesses solidified, and mindsets established. Your ability to immerse yourself in an existing team, engage with members in a positive way, and draw a great performance from them will be the determining factors in your success as a leader. And while some of the steps required for success here are similar to those outlined in the previous chapter, there are also some unique factors to consider when taking the helm of an existing team.

Here are six things to consider when assuming a leadership role with an existing team. Some of these points will feel and sound similar to the last chapter, but that's intentional. When you inherit a new team to lead, there are some similarities to building a brand new team… and some differences also:

1. **Be clear on goals—yours and the team's.** Having goals is paramount to reaching any successful outcome. In the early days with an inherited team, it may take some time for appropriate goals to materialize. Be patient and maintain focus until they come into focus.

   In this case, you need to think about two kinds of goals: your own and the team's. Are you trying to achieve a quick turnaround? Reach a short- or medium-term milestone and then move on to another assignment? Or are you planning to lead the team for a while? Will you need to build things in a more durable way? Your personal goals may dictate how aggressively you should refashion the team. And, as with any team, it's important to understand what the group's goals will be so that you and others can gauge success and progress. Perhaps you will consult with others on these goals. Perhaps you will design them on your own. That will depend on your style and the situation, but a little collaboration with others never hurts.

2. **Detail the skills, behaviors, rules, and expectations you have for your new team, and communicate them.** Whenever we lead or manage a team, it's important to be clear about a few things above and beyond goals. We need to understand the qualities we'd like to have on our team: the skills the team members need to have, the behaviors we expect them to exhibit, and the rules and expectations we intend to instill. These things will create the structure for the team and will also provide a road map for conduct, decision making, problem resolution, and structure on the team.

   When we are building a brand-new team, we may have the time to deal with each one of these areas (skills, behaviors, rules, and expectations) separately. When we inherit an existing team, we may need to make decisions and plan more quickly. We may need to abbreviate some of this planning. But regardless of how much we do, there is still great value in spending at least *some* time thinking about and making decisions on these types of issues.

Taking this step with an inherited team will help you create alignment with this team in the short term, and it will also give you a framework to help you (quietly) plan for the team's evolution over the long term. In other words, this framework will help you determine who fits and should stay and who should be moved on to something else. You'll be able to begin making decisions on the changes you might need to make, and the skills and behaviors you need to look for in new team members.

3.  **Focus on earning trust and credibility.** When building a team from the ground up, you have a major opportunity—and responsibility—to establish good rapport with team members. When building a team from the ground up, you can bring on people with whom you have an existing positive relationship. You can build something together and allow team members to contribute to the design of the project, the team, or their roles. You can grow together as a team, and that usually creates some trust and credibility. The existence of trust and credibility is always important.[57]

    But when you inherit an existing team to lead, trust and credibility are much harder to earn and maintain. Perhaps the people on the team don't know you. Perhaps you are new not only to the team, but also to the organization. Perhaps someone on the team wanted the leadership position for himself or herself. Perhaps there was dysfunction or underperformance prior to your arrival and the esprit de corps is low. There are many possible roadblocks to your ability to build trust and credibility

---

[57]Key Concept #7: Trust and credibility are the keys to the castle—especially when you inherit an existing team to lead. When you can build a team from the ground up, if you lead well, and collaborate with the people around you, trust and credibility grow organically. But with an inherited team, it's much harder to create that trust, and your window of opportunity to build that trust is much smaller. Leading an existing, inherited team requires specific focus.

with your new team. But you must, must, *must* focus a great deal of energy here. How do we build trust and credibility? Well, that's almost an entire book topic unto itself. But here are a few things to think about now:

- It's always good to ask questions and actually listen to the answers. Let people tell you what they think. Don't do all the talking.

- Match your actions and your words. Do what you say you will do.

- Speak with people, not at them.

4.  **Build as much consensus and ownership as possible.** This point is often overlooked, but it's just as important as the others. You should always think about ways to build consensus on the goals of the team and the plan for the future. In the process, you will create ownership. You want the members of your team to *own* what happens, because when they feel a sense of ownership, they will be more engaged, more passionate, and more effective in their work. We need to get our teams to own the outcome, own the process, and own the future of the team. We need them to care. It's easier to create this with a new team, but it's just as critical, if not more so, with an existing team.

    How do we create ownership with an inherited team? Start by asking a few questions of the team, as soon as you take over, and give them the freedom to comment openly:

    - What goals do we have in place? Are they the correct goals?

    - What's been working with the team so far? What can we do better?

    - What hasn't been working? What should we do less of?

    - What would you do if you were in charge of this team?

    These questions are really all asking the same thing: "What do you think?" Asking this question—and listening to the answers—is a surefire way to earn trust and credibility.

Once you begin asking those "What do you think?" questions, you will then need to begin managing expectations. Why? Because once you start asking people what they think, they might expect that they will get what they want. You want people to feel like they have a seat at the table, they have a voice, and their opinion is at least sought out. Seeking opinions will help you build credibility. But you will quickly lose that credibility if people's expectations aren't met and they do not get what they suggested or asked for all the time. To build that trust and credibility, we need to ask for opinions, heed those opinions at least some of the time, and manage the expectation that they will be heeded all of the time.

Trust and credibility will only last as long as you continue to earn them. They are not limitless. Your reserve needs to be nurtured and tended to, always. Even if you earn some initial credibility by asking questions, it will wither away if your actions don't eventually justify it.

Trust and credibility are the most important currency in team building. Period.

5.  **Create your plan for change.** The common denominator of the first four points in this list is that you need to understand your team and get it functioning as well as possible, as quickly as possible. But at the same time, while getting the team quickly aligned and organized, you may also realize that some pieces of the team that you inherited are not a good fit. You may have to contend with people who don't want to be a part of the team you are trying to create, who don't agree with your vision, who don't share the sandbox well with others. Depending on the length of time you plan to be the leader of the group, you may need to map out a plan to upgrade the team around you by asking questions such as the following:

    • Who fits your vision, meets the criteria, and should stay?

- Who adds some value but is not a perfect fit?
  - Can that person have his or her role adjusted within the team?
  - Who needs to be moved on entirely to something else?
- Over what timeframe do you want or need to have these changes made?

It's important to have a plan in place to restructure and improve the team around you.

6. **Play the hand you have been dealt.** While you need to map out your upgrade plan, you also need to play the game with the cards you've been dealt. Sometimes we are simply stuck with certain aspects of our inherited team and need to learn to lead, manage, and maximize output with less-than-ideal resources. You probably won't be able to make massive change immediately. Your new team will have to begin to function and be productive, with change happening over time. So you should be thinking about maximizing the team's productivity in the short term while change emerges over the medium and long term.

As I wrote above, some of these steps are similar to the ones you might take when building a brand-new team. But the context is different with an inherited team: While a certain step might be similar, the ways in which you implement that step are quite different. We need to think differently when we inherit an existing team to lead.

Teams are a fascinating study in human behavior. While leadership is about many things, at its core it is about getting groups of people to work together and do the things you or your organization needs them to do. When we can assemble our team from its inception, it is often easier to achieve this. But when we inherit bits and pieces from previous leaders and situations, the work becomes much harder.

Perhaps the ultimate sign of good leadership is the ability to motivate thaa preexisting team to be productive with you.

# SHARING THE SANDBOX

## chapter 13: managing extreme personalities

*Build for your team a feeling of oneness, of dependence
on one another, and of strength to be derived by unity.*

**– Vince Lombardi**

Building and leading great teams requires, at its most elemental level, a strong understanding of people. Teams are nothing more than a collection of individuals, and individuals are emotionally complex. Building great teams and great organizations often requires that we understand the types of personalities of the individuals on our teams, especially the extreme ones. These extreme personalities typically create the biggest leadership challenges, so understanding them can really boost the success of the team.[58]

In this chapter we will detail some extreme personality profiles that occur frequently enough to be called "archetypes." And, just as importantly, we'll discuss some ways that you can effectively deal with each one.

We divide these archetypes into a few macro groups:

---

[58]Key Concept #8: Extreme personalities must be managed, and they usually take up a disproportionate amount of your leadership time. Having a strategy to deal with certain common, problematic personality archetypes will save you time and help you keep the team on track.

1.  **The Emotionalists**, who distract their teams and teammates by drawing attention with overly demonstrative, emotional behavior and evoking emotional responses from those around them.

2.  **The Individualists**, who are known for their self-centeredness. These archetypes can cause significant distractions within their teams because their actions (and perhaps their words) make it clear to all that they are more interested in their own goals than the team's.

3.  **The Survivalists**, who can be less overt than other personality types, but are just as insidious. They share the common denominator of low productivity and lack of accountability, and they can be distracting because they are not viewed as carrying their fair share of the workload. They frequently sidestep accountability.

Archetypes are universal. But in reality, personality traits frequently manifest themselves in degrees; rarely are they all-or-nothing. Those with archetypal personalities sometimes shed those characteristics. Likewise, non-archetypal team members sometimes adopt a few of these characteristics temporarily. But regardless of whether a person often or seldom fits the profile, it will be helpful to understand how to manage these behaviors when you encounter them.

## The Emotionalists

These four personality archetypes are bound together by their use of emotion to get what they want (often attention). In many, if not most, of their professional interactions, they complicate situations by responding emotionally.

**The Dramatist.** The Dramatist craves attention. Real issues in his life (deaths in the family, sickness, disappointments, events, and so forth) are accompanied by great public displays of emotion.[59] Extreme Dramatists may even go so far as to create issues where none exist in order to draw even more attention to themselves.

Drama can be a major distraction for any team. Some teammates will feed into it and fawn over a Dramatist. Others will openly resent the Dramatist for distracting the team. It's hard for people to ignore Dramatists, especially the "talented" ones, who know how to create drama that is hard to ignore. Nearly everyone on your team will be drawn into the emotional center, the Dramatist will attract lots of energy, and voilà: mission accomplished for the Dramatist. No matter what the specifics of the situation are, the Dramatist's presence fosters dysfunction.

The best strategy for dealing with the Dramatist is to avoid feeding the beast:

1. Don't contribute to or encourage his behavior by providing the attention he seeks.

2. Keep your interactions purely professional and friendly.

3. Don't ask, "What's wrong?" every time you see a sad look or a furrowed brow. If you are the team leader, quietly encourage the team to do the same.

4. Don't allow the Dramatist's personal issues to become topics of group discussion. Just keep the focus on business.

5. If an issue becomes particularly distracting, gently speak to the Dramatist privately and remind him to keep personal issues out of the workplace.

These steps won't necessarily change who or what The Dramatist is. But they will help you manage the damage or distraction to your team.

**The Delicate Flower.** Delicate Flowers are often good hearted with good intentions and little desire to disrupt. At the same time, they

[59]This can take many forms: the constant occurrence of personal problems that are brought into the workplace; loud, emotional phone calls held within earshot of colleagues; the obvious expressions of sadness that are clearly meant to elicit sympathy; or maybe the open-ended, somewhat vague comments like "life sucks" that are meant to draw you into a conversation about his personal issues. I'm sure you can think of other examples as well.

are emotionally fragile. Their egos require constant maintenance. They crave positive feedback and react very emotionally when confronted with blame or constructive criticism.

Honest feedback, especially in public, is nearly impossible with this personality. It is often hard to get at the root of any problem because as soon as you begin to suggest one exists, the highly emotional, defensive reaction that results is often more distracting than the problem itself. Once teammates recognize this behavior, they will see this person as a roadblock to progress.

Delicate Flowers require a great deal of time to manage correctly:

1.  Consider everything you say to them before you say it, and assume everything you say will be taken in a way other than how it was intended.

2.  Manage the Delicate Flower's ego and guide her emotional responses through frequent positive feedback, even for things that may seem meaningless. Doing so will allow you to offer negative feedback in a positive way by gently saying, "You've done these things well. Let's look at ways we might do this one thing a bit better."

3.  Team leaders need to be prepared to spend a lot of energy keeping the train running on the tracks with this personality, because if it derails, it may take some time to get going again.

**The Scorekeeper.** This personality keeps a mental score with his teammates, business partners, even clients or customers—anyone who has wronged him in some way. Scorekeepers are sensitive to perceived insults, slights, and affronts and have very long memories. What's more, they often look for ways to even the score, sometimes even years after an alleged incident. Some Scorekeepers will even brag about this list or dangle it in front of others as if to say, "Don't mess with me; you don't want to end up on my list." Their methods are subversive, and their ability to triangulate situations can be divisive and destructive.

Once the Scorekeeper's teammates become aware of his personality traits, they often adopt one of two common reactions: Some will steer clear, not wanting to risk crossing him, and might give the Score-keeper what he wants just because it is safer. This is exactly the reaction the Scorekeeper wants. The second common reaction people have is resentment. In this case, teammates become adversaries as they look for ways to cross swords with the Scorekeeper. Neither one is good. You either have people avoiding confrontation and settling for less-than-ideal solutions to issues, or you have people focused more on waging war than actually getting good work done.

There a few key strategies for managing a Scorekeeper:

1. Guide him toward professionalism in all his interactions. With-out directly addressing the Scorekeeper by name, discuss scorekeeping behaviors as being unprofessional. In other words, try to avoid the direct confrontation first.

2. If the indirect approach does not work, it is important to call out scorekeeping behaviors when you see them. (Doing so pri-vately, but directly, is usually most effective.)

3. Above all, professional retribution from the Scorekeeper can-not be tolerated, and if quiet coaching is ineffective, you may need to take more extreme steps to change the behavior, such as a formal review and intervention with a superior.

**The Disruptive Contrarian.** The Disruptive Contrarian likes to ar-gue. She takes the opposite side of every issue within your team re-gardless of her personal opinion. You can predict her stance on issues with relative precision based on how the rest of the group thinks. But Disruptive Contrarians do more than just disagree. They disagree in dis-agreeable ways. They agitate other members of the team by seemingly disagreeing just to disagree. They sometimes offer a valid counterpoint but most often have nothing substantial to contribute.

The problem with Disruptive Contrarians is that your team will end up discussing issues emotionally—rather than logically. While there is great value in having a teammate who positively and respectfully plays devil's advocate, the Disruptive Contrarian becomes a distraction with a point of view that eventually no one will consider.

There are two ways to deal with a Disruptive Contrarian:

1.  One is to engage her on the issues, bring her "inside," seek her counsel. Make her feel like part of the process (if you think she has something to contribute).

2.  The alternative, if you don't see any positive role for the Disruptive Contrarian, is to marginalize her. Limit her negative impact on the group by keeping her out of the loop on issues. This is a short-term solution, however, because the Disruptive Contrarian will almost certainly not react well to being ignored and will create additional distractions through her frustrations.

### Summary of the Emotionalists

While the ideal strategy for dealing with an Emotionalist archetypal team member may be to remove the person, often this is not an immediate option. Team leaders need to have strategies for minimizing the negative impact on team performance. When it comes to Emotionalists, the best strategy is to remove emotion from your own reactions whenever possible. Respond calmly. Try to keep the focus on professional activities, and avoid engaging these archetypes on the level that they consciously or unconsciously seek. In some cases, the extra emotion *can* be used for a positive outcome. Perhaps the extra emotion can be channeled into a part of the organization that is moribund or deflated. But that extra emotion always comes with great risk that needs to be managed. Tread carefully.

## The Individualists

This group of four personality archetypes is connected by their desire to either distance themselves from the group, or to build themselves up by putting others down. The Individualists are not interested in easily conforming into the team. They are interested in doing their own thing first, with the success of the team coming in a distant second.

**The Lone Ranger.** This personality usually has either of the following: an excess of confidence in himself or an almost total lack of confidence in those around him. Regardless, the net result is the same. This personality will always choose to get the job done alone rather than work with others. To be fair, the Lone Ranger may simply communicate poorly or may be shy, or he may be exceptionally good at doing his job or may have little patience. There are many potential reasons for a Lone Ranger's preference for individual work, but the bottom line is that he prefers to work alone.

This personality is a problem because one person working alone may cause others to want to do the same. The Lone Ranger may incite resentment in others because, in their minds, "this was supposed to be a team, and some of us are not acting like it." Problems may also arise if the Lone Ranger fails to seek input or build any consensus.

There are many possible consequences of having a Lone Ranger on a team, few of them good. The worst-case scenario for a manager would be a Lone Ranger who triggers resentment, but who, at the same time, is highly productive. Having talent is always good. But talent in one who causes significant problems, underperformance, or dysfunction in others may be a net negative.

Here are a few thoughts on dealing with a Lone Ranger:

1.  Determine how much value he actually adds. Disruption without significant value added is one thing. But disruption with high productivity is another thing entirely. If your Lone Ranger adds great value, think carefully before shaking things up too much.

2.  Some people legitimately work better alone, and the great manager should determine if this is the case. That determination should then dictate how far "back to the pack" the manager should bring the Lone Ranger.

3.  It usually needs to be made clear to the Lone Ranger that he should work more or better with teammates. This will take repeated conversations and managerial effort. But if the Lone Ranger adds great value, the leader must also explain to the team that this person's style of productivity is good for all.

**The Ego.** This personality is a slight variation on the Lone Ranger, but the differences make the Ego even more destructive and divisive. Egos think they are smarter, better, and faster than everyone else and are not afraid to say so (even when their perspective is not based on reality). This personality thinks little of others and thinks very highly of the person in the mirror.

The Ego is a problem in some of the same ways as the Lone Ranger, but with a biting edge. Lone Rangers may operate demurely, while Egos are frequently loud and highly offensive. They are not satisfied with just working alone. They need everyone else to know that they are better, and they accomplish this by being critical of others.

While you may want to give a productive Lone Ranger some leeway, you will usually need to put the Ego in check. This isn't easy because the Ego almost always thinks that she is smarter and better than the leader of the team in addition to all its members. (The worst case is when the Ego actually is smarter or better than the rest.[60]) A good goal with an Ego is to attempt to transition her into a Lone Ranger and try to get her to do less damage to others in the process of performing at a high level. Doing so can at least minimize the criticism or damage to others, which in itself is significant progress.

**The Politician.** This personality is a little too smooth, too slick, too friendly, and too enthusiastic—a little too everything. Consequently, others on the team start to believe that the Politician has an alternate agenda. Teammates may or may not know what that agenda is, but they are sure it is there.

The possibility of an alternate agenda always creates discomfort and distrust among team members. Lines of communication are strained, trust erodes, and the team dynamic breaks down. Great teams are built on, among other things, a high level of trust. People won't trust a teammate who is suspected of having an alternate agenda.

---

[60] It is always harder to manage an Ego who is legitimately smarter, more productive, or more successful than everyone else around her. This sort of overly confident yet incredibly talented person may have the potential to be the superstar of the team. The hardest part will be to get her to continue to produce while also understanding that there is no value in hurting others. Even though this Ego may carry a disproportionate share of the productivity load, the good team leader will find ways (even little ones) to demonstrate that others do contribute in a way that helps the Ego. The more legitimately talented the Ego is, the harder it will be to deal with her successfully.

Dealing with a Politician is tricky. You never quite know what the agenda might be, and there is also a chance that there is not an alternate agenda at work; perhaps the Politician is simply a little too "slick" for his own good. The best advice on dealing with this personality: Always be wary, but as long as the Politician is being productive, tread lightly. If the problem manifests itself into distracting dysfunction among teammates, however, you may need to bring people together and encourage communication around common goals, plans, team agendas, etc. In other words, if the presence of the Politician is taking a toll on trust within your team, you may have to facilitate the rebuilding of that trust through team dialogue.

**The Self Promoter.** This personality is to the Politician as the Ego is to the Lone Ranger. While teammates may not know what the Politician's agenda is, they know full well the Self Promoter's: personal advancement. With the Politician, you merely suspect that there is something else going on; with the Self Promoter, you know there is.

This personality is a problem because everyone on the team knows that the agenda is not about team advancement, it's about personal advancement. This causes intense frustration and dysfunction within the team. The Self Promoter causes one of two things to happen: teammates begin to compete for their own advancement[61] or else they withdraw from the team dynamic entirely out of frustration. Regardless, the Self Promoter can be one of the most destructive forces on your team and cannot be ignored. If you ignore the impact of the Self Promoter and others on the team see this happen, you will almost certainly be seen as a weak leader who allowed a bad situation to worsen.[62]

---

[61] Once others on the team feel like the Self Promoter is actively seeking advancement for herself, everyone's own ambitions will kick in, and they won't want to get left behind. This could create an everyone-for-themselves dynamic. In this case, you'll end up with a group of people fighting for themselves rather than any semblance of a team.

[62] One of the great examples of a Self Promoter from the world of sports was Dennis Rodman, who played for several teams in the NBA and was part of two great teams: the Detroit Pistons of the early 1990s and the Chicago Bulls of the mid-1990s. In his early years in Detroit, Rodman was a secondary, but highly talented, character on two championship teams. But then he became seemingly obsessed with building the reputation and brand of Dennis Rodman as an extreme personality, always seeking attention through outrageous behavior and hard partying. He quickly became known as a cancerous presence on a team. That is, until he came to the Chicago Bulls and under the tutelage of Phil Jackson. Coach Jackson successfully integrated Rodman and his self-promoting ways into an already successful team with one of the strongest personalities we have ever seen in sports: Michael Jordan. While I certainly wasn't inside the Bull's locker room, I've read enough of Coach Jackson's writings to know that his strategy to get Rodman to conform enough to deal with him privately, never challenge Rodman's fragile ego publicly, and to constantly sell Rodman on how the success of the team actually benefitted Rodman as an individual.

There are a few key ways to deal with a Self Promoter:

1.  Deal with the Self Promoter head on, with specifics, and in private.

2.  Arm yourself with examples of her self-promotional behavior and how it hurts the team.

3.  Focus your conversations on how damage to the team hurts the Self Promoter as well. The Self Promoter is wired to think in terms of personal gain, so try explaining the negative cause-and-effect cycle of her behavior in terms of how it is self-defeating. The Self Promoter will understand that.

**Summary of the Individualists**

Dealing with Individualists can be tricky, because often the destructive behavior is hard to detect and even harder to interpret. But when individualist tendencies are detected, the best strategy usually involves explaining to the Individualists the benefits of working more or being more productive within the construct of the team. Individualists tend to think of things in terms of their own gain or loss. If we can successfully translate their behaviors into those terms, so they understand what is at stake, we have a higher likelihood of bringing them back into the team dynamic.

# The Survivalists

Finally, let's look at four extreme personalities that can be a little less obvious. With the common denominator of low productivity and lack of accountability, these archetypes can cause major distractions within their teams because they are not viewed as carrying their fair share of the workload. We call these four the Survivalists because they all are able to sidestep accountability and avoid being called to task for low performance.

**The Free Rider.** This person is always around, but no one is quite sure what he actually does. If you ask others in the office what the Free Rider is responsible for, most will struggle to answer. This personality's actual portfolio of work isn't that big, yet he always seems to avoid taking on more work. When asked by a colleague what he is working on, the Free Rider always has lots to say. He is the master of sounding and looking industrious. But in reality, he is not.

As we discussed in an earlier chapter, the current economy has forced most companies to become lean and mean. Everyone is being asked to do more work for the same money. In other words, there is plenty of work to be done, and in most organizations, there is little room for people to be carrying less than their fair share of the load. Therefore, when there is someone on the team who is doing less, the team can quickly become dysfunctional. Once the Free Rider has been "outed," people realize he is just really good at avoiding work, and he becomes a very divisive figure.

Here are a few good strategies for dealing with the Free Rider:

1.  Be very specific about your expectations of the scope and timelines for completion of his tasks.

2.  Try micromanaging him closely for a while to make sure that work is being done and accountability is clear. I rarely recommend micromanagement as a leadership style, but in some extreme cases (like this one) it will often be the best approach.

3.  Write down a clear job description with clear responsibilities and expectations. Review it frequently until you are sure the Free Rider is doing his fair share.

**The Buck Passer.** This Survivalist differs from the Free Rider in the sense that she does plenty of work. But what makes the Buck Passer a potential problem is that she resists taking responsibility for anything that may go wrong. She will rarely, if ever, raise her hand and say she's accountable for anything. She'll work on it, she'll partner with you, but she'll always stop short of taking ultimate responsibility.

This personality is an issue because no one wants to partner with someone who refuses to be on the hook for anything. People who avoid accountability and try to blend into the background when things go wrong are not good teammates. When it becomes obvious that there is a Buck Passer on the team, others can become less willing to raise their hands and take responsibility. In this way, buck passing can become contagious and, eventually, toxic.

The strategy for dealing with the Buck Passer is similar to that for the Free Rider, at least in the short term:

1.  Be very specific in your communications and expectations.

2.  Require that the Buck Passer take some accountability, and help her realize that simply doing work is not enough—there must also be accountability.

**The Committee Man (or Woman).** When key decisions are made, this personality always seems to be in the room, on the call, or part of the committee. And because this personality always seems to be "on the inside," he often gets the good assignments and avoids the bad ones. The Committee Man often remains entrenched in a position long after his value to the organization has dropped. Because of the length of his service, his institutional knowledge may make him valuable, but this knowledge usually obscures the fact that he just doesn't do that much actual work.

The Committee Man often lingers long past his sell-by date—and this entrenchment can limit the growth of up-and-coming talent. Leading good teams often requires keeping people fresh in their positions, and the presence of the Committee Man, who is just going through the motions, can become a major pipeline blocker.

The strategies for managing the Committee Man are as follows:

1.  Leverage the residual value of his institutional knowledge without blocking the growth of the team. You need the Committee Man to be more than just an oracle of organizational information. Everyone, Committee Man included, needs to do some actual work.

2.  In some organizations, it may make sense to have term limits for certain positions so that you can avoid having the same people in the same roles for too long.

3. Good leaders will consider moving people around, not so often as to be disruptive, but often enough to keep things fresh.

4. Consider setting up the Committee Man as a mentor for young talent. His institutional knowledge may be valuable, but his presence should not inhibit growth and development.

**The Theorist.** This personality loves the big idea but hates the big work. She is very vocal in her creativity, always suggesting better ways to do things, but when it comes time to actually roll up her sleeves and get the job done, the Theorist always seems to lag behind the others. Moreover, the Theorist usually comes up with ideas that sound great but are completely impractical to execute.

This personality is a problem because others on the team will quickly identify the Theorist for what she is, and they will then tune out her grand ideas. No one wants to be teammates with someone who is all talk and no action. Sure, some creativity and big thinking can be valuable. But grand ideas must be accompanied by some practical execution, especially in a market environment like this one, when budgets are tight and the allocation of every resource is scrutinized.

The strategy for managing the Theorist is specificity:

1. Require that she add practicality to her creativity.

2. Whenever she approaches you with something new, listen if you have the time and are interested, but then insist that she give you specifics on how to bring her idea to life.

3. Push her to go beyond the idea itself and actually include some practical planning.

## Summary of the Survivalists

In each of these cases, your strategy is similar. You need to be specific with the Survivalists, and encourage accountability, planning, and practicality. Some personality types like Emotionalists and Individualists can be divisive because they are offensive and aggressive with their teammates. But Survivalists are all divisive because, above all else, they fail to carry their own weight or actively contribute to the outcome of the team. This behavior incites resentment in those around them. Everyone needs to do their fair share of the work and take their fair share of the responsibility.

Managing extreme personalities like the Survivalists is not easy, because you may be forced to get more engaged in the specifics of their day-to-day work than you would prefer. But if you manage these personalities well, eventually you may be able to improve their behavior and reduce their divisiveness within your team.

These extreme personality archetypes are a challenge to manage, and if not managed well, they will create situations that are divisive and ultimately destructive to the team dynamic you have worked so hard to build. While I don't recommend pre-judging people, I do suggest keeping a keen eye out for certain behavior patterns and doing some initial planning on how you will deal with certain types of extreme behavior. If we don't manage these types of behavior patterns well, they will suck up a disproportionate amount of your time and energy and make your team-leadership job much harder.

# SHARING THE SANDBOX

chapter 14: when things fall apart

*A primary reason capable people fail to advance
is that they don't work well with their colleagues.*

**– Lee Iacocca**

Sometimes, no matter how hard we try, our team just doesn't thrive. Sometimes it fails completely. Team members may fall short of delivering what we thought they would deliver, or our team may end up a bubbling cauldron of dysfunction, rather than that smooth cocktail we were hoping for. Sometimes the realities of the situation simply overwhelm the team. Sometimes *it just doesn't work out.*

We can take all the right steps at the outset, do all the necessary planning, and assemble a team and plan a project in the most diligent way, and it still may not work out the way we want it to. What do you do as a team leader when success is no longer possible but failure is not an option?[63]

For one thing, you can make a point of asking yourself every once in a while, "What will I do if this team fails? How will I respond? How will I attempt to save the situation?" If you game out these scenarios

---

[63] Key Concept #9: What will you do if things fall apart? No matter how good a leader you are or how much time you spend thinking about and building your teams, sometimes it just doesn't work out.

once in a while, you'll be better prepared to respond if they actually do happen.

Here are a few ideas to consider when things go awry:

1.  **Take a look in the mirror.** Examine your own behaviors. Ask some trusted teammates or advisors to evaluate you. Ask yourself what you can and should be doing differently. You may realize that you are the problem. At a minimum, you may come up with some concrete ways to improve your own performance, and when other members of the team see you looking in the mirror, they are more likely to do the same for themselves.

2.  **Go back to your planning and preparation.** In chapters 11 and 12, we laid out a series of first steps you should take as you plan and build your team. Those steps are critical, and not just in the preparatory stages. All that work you did around goals, roles, and responsibilities can serve you well when things start to fall apart. Here's a perfect example. My wife teaches at a private boarding school in our home state of Connecticut. I do a little work with some of her school's sports teams and coaching staffs, including the coaching staff of the boys' hockey team. Several years ago, we tried having the players write out team goals and expectations at the beginning of the season, and then sign the document. The team relied on that agreement to dictate the culture of the team, but, more importantly, it has helped avoid a number of problems as seasons have progressed. How? Well, each time the team hits a rough patch, the team's leaders pull out the document and review with team members what they previously agreed to. This exercise provides the team with a calm, unemotional way to look in the mirror and remind each other what they had decided they wanted to be. Does it solve every problem? Of course not. But it can solve a lot of them. If you do your planning correctly at the outset, you not only start off on the right foot, but you also

establish a framework for resolving disputes and overcoming challenges.[64]

3. **Communicate as directly as possible.** Problems ignored don't disappear. On the contrary, they tend to become bigger and harder to solve as time goes by. When things on your team start to malfunction, it's usually best to deal with the issues directly. You might need to start by speaking privately with certain team members to find out what is going on. Perhaps you then have some group dialogue. Perhaps you communicate with the subset of the team that is causing or having the problem. Perhaps you deal with the problem gently. Perhaps you deal with it harshly. All of these possibilities depend on the gravity and nature of the problem. The point here is that you will do better, more often, if you put issues on the table, talk about them, and attempt to work through them. A problem ignored almost always becomes a problem that you regret ignoring.

4. **Look for other leaders on the team.** People like to see themselves as leaders, as reliable resources to help solve problems. So, when you are on a team that is starting to falter, consider appealing to the leadership instincts of some of the key members. Bring them inside, talk to them about how you need their help to solve the problem. Appeal to their sense of pride and ownership over the team and its productivity. This concept is related to your preparation of your team. If you create a sense of ownership at the outset, you can put this to use when things go south. People will care more about things they feel they own.

5. **Avoid using embarrassment.** If there is a person on your team who is causing the problem, embarrassing them publicly

---

[64]In a business setting, you can plan out how your team will handle potential pitfalls. Ask yourself questions like these: How will we react if we miss our deadlines and the project goes off track? How will we handle the emotions if one of us gets the big promotion we all want? How will we deal with a teammate who starts to drift away from the team and pursue a personal agenda? If you do this, you have a good chance of being ready when challenges arise.

rarely provides the results you seek. When you have an under-performer on your team, your goal should be to get him or her realigned with the team, carrying his or her own weight. Embarrassment rarely achieves this. Conversely, it usually drives a wedge deeper between the underperformer and the rest of the team.

6. **Make changes when you need to.** Sometimes, no matter how hard we try, no matter what we do, we end up with a group of parts that don't fit. And sometimes all the effort in the world won't change that fact. When it becomes undeniable that you have a team that isn't going to work, the only move is to make a change. Someone may have to go. The entire team may have to go. Sometimes even the leader—yes, you!—may have to go.[65] Regardless of the shift that needs to take place, changing your team takes courage and confidence. If you have exhausted all other possibilities and the performance of the team remains at risk, making a change is the only option.

7. **Remember the lessons learned for the next time.** Every team experience flows into the next one. Every team and every team situation is different. It follows that every team opportunity is, above all else, a new opportunity to learn how to lead, manage, and follow better. Whether your team experience ends well or poorly, take note of what worked and what didn't. Begin building a toolbox of techniques you can use to do better next time.

Despite hard work and planning, sometimes things just don't work out. Good team planning requires that we not only plan when constructing the team, but that we also have a contingency plan when

---

[65] Perhaps the hardest part of leadership is to accept that sometimes you, the leader, are the problem. This runs contrary to so many natural leadership instincts, and it is the rare person who can lead with conviction and vision (and the innate confidence that requires) and who also has the humility to know when to step away. I think the key here is that when things go wrong on your team, have the confidence to ask yourself, and perhaps one or two key, trusted advisors, "Am I part of the problem?" The leader who will never even entertain that possibility will almost always eventually become part of the problem. Great leaders aren't afraid to look in the mirror once in a while and examine their own behaviors.

things start to go badly. Each team experience flows into the next, so if we can do a good job exiting a bad situation, we may actually facilitate a good entry into the next one.

# SHARING THE SANDBOX

chapter 15: playbooks

*If you don't have time to do it right, when will you have time to do it over?*
**– John Wooden**

The word "team" applies to many different types of groups of people—especially in the 21st-century workplace, where technology has given us constant access to anyone anywhere in the world. The concept of "team" has therefore become more complicated, with more groups of people able to work together than ever before. So let's look at a few of the most common variations and discuss some additional ways to make them productive. Remember, every person is unique, so every *team* is unique. Adjust your thinking accordingly.

## The Virtual Team

A Virtual Team is a team that is spread out over many locations, connected by the wonders of electronic communication. The hardest part of the Virtual Team is that the group rarely sees each other face to face, and in many cases, team members have never met in person. Despite an abundance of tools that make it easy to communicate remotely, human beings still collaborate best when they are in the same room.

So how do you cause people who are geographically remote to feel connected to each other and the team? It's not easy, but there are a few strategies that can make a big difference. The common denominator with all of these steps is increased communication. Lacking the casual, random communication of a conventional office, leaders of virtual teams need to jump-start such interactions for their team members. Here's how.

1.  **Help team members learn about each other:**

    - Hold "get to know each other" phone calls when the team is newly formed, wherein people tell some things about themselves that are non-work-related, and that no one else on the team knows.

    - Create a list of biographies, roles, and responsibilities, and have the bios include things beyond the workplace.

    - Find ways to get everyone on the team talking and contributing in each virtual meeting, so everyone feels like they are part of something. Pick a topic and ask everyone to comment on it. Pair people up who never work together, ask them to learn about each other, and then have them each introduce their partner to the others in the group. There are lots of ways to accomplish this.

2.  **Give frequent updates on team plans and progress.** A good Virtual Team leader communicates more frequently than usual in the early life of the Virtual Team. The leader will communicate on decisions that are made, the reasons they were made, and the implications. The good leader will communicate the path on which leadership is taking the team, and why that path is the correct one. Frequent communication from team

leadership has the dual benefit of strengthening members' connections to the team and boosting leader credibility.[66]

3. **Schedule in-person meetings.** There is great benefit in planning occasional face-to-face gatherings for your team. Even if it only happens once a year, an in-person team gathering will go a long way toward building bonds.

4. **Use video conferencing, not just voice.** Leverage the benefit of the visual connection. If people can see each other, and put faces with names and voices, that will strengthen connections among the team.[67]

## The Cross-Functional Team

The Cross-Functional Team is challenging to lead, simply because it is a broad group of people from different areas of the company. These people might even come from different industries. They might not know each other at all, might be meeting for the first time, might have little understanding about what the other people on the team do. There might be a lack of appreciation for the skills and responsibilities of others on the team. It's important, therefore, to get the members of the Cross-Functional Team to do more than get to know each other. They also need to understand the needs of all the members, including what will stress a teammate out, and what a teammate needs to be successful.

---

[66] I lived this one personally. When I became Chairman of the US Olympic Sailing Program in October 2004, there was a distinct trust and credibility gap within the program. Athletes did not trust leadership, staff was frustrated, and the esprit de corps was low. The new leadership team we brought in had big plans to improve the program, but the athletes did not know what those plans were and had no reason yet to trust the new leadership. Most of the athletes knew me as a former fellow Olympic sailor, but not in a leadership capacity.

So I began sending a monthly e-mail to everyone in the program, giving updates on what was happening and why, and communicating on the direction in which we were taking the team. Did everyone read these communications? Certainly not. But many did. And the e-mail communications were a big part of the increased sense of team and trust that we have built over the last several years.

After the 2008 Olympic Games, when it was obvious that a healthy amount of trust had been restored, I scaled back the monthly communications and now distribute these "directional" messages on a less-frequent basis. And with decreased supply, I think the interest and demand for a message from leadership has actually increased.

[67] Here's a perfect example. Are you more likely to be rude to someone next to you, but in another car, or to someone standing next to you in line at the store? Obviously the barrier of separate cars makes it easier to be rude because you lack any sort of personal connection. When we can build personal connections and create environments where people have to deal with each other directly, it's harder for people to be rude to each other.

1. **Clarify roles and responsibilities.** Clarity in this area is important for any team, but it is especially so with the Cross-Functional Team. Understanding the roles also will help the members of the team get to know and understand each other better. The good Cross-Functional Team leader will facilitate extensive knowledge sharing and communication in this area, well above and beyond simply exchanging job descriptions.

2. **Facilitate dialogue.** Try generating communications that will help people understand each other better, such as "what can teammates do to help you succeed?" or "what things do we need to know about you and your role?" or "what should we avoid so as not to annoy you?" It might take more time, but extra effort in this area will be rewarded.

### The Global Team

Different native languages and cultural norms are major roadblocks to a successful Global Team. To get around this, a Global Team leader should promote the sharing of cultural knowledge.

1. **Create a sense of respect for other cultures, as well as for other people.** With the Global Team, you need to do more than just get to know your teammates. You also need to get to know the cultures of your teammates. Things are perceived differently in different cultures; an action that might be a compliment in one culture could be an insult in another.[68] This extra layer of knowledge will serve you well and will be a sign of great respect to others. Depending on the culture, you may need to consider an adjustment to the way you introduce yourself, the amount of eye contact you use, the way you speak and interact in meetings, where you sit, the way you treat the senior or junior people in the room. There are many potential adjust-

---

[68]For example, direct eye contact is perceived to show confidence and inspire trust in many western cultures, but in some Asian cultures, the same amount of eye contact can be perceived as aggressive and even insulting.

ments.[69] The more sensitive we are to cultural perceptions, the more successful we will be in a global environment.

I am not recommending that everyone become an expert on world culture. But a little effort and information can go a long way. And if you can increase cultural awareness on your Global Team, you will be creating the culture of respect we have mentioned so many times in *Sharing the Sandbox*.

2.  **If the team communicates in your native language, make it easy for people to understand you.** I studied French in school, and at one point could have survived (barely) in a French-speaking environment. During this time, I noticed that my ability to communicate and understand others improved dramatically if the French speaker used simple language (spoken slowly, with few colloquialisms). If he or she started speaking rapidly and in a more complex way, I couldn't keep up. I try to remember this when conversing with nonnative speakers.

    If you are on a global team operating primarily in your native language, remember to make these adjustments:

    *   Speak more slowly to compensate for the fact that some people might need time to mentally translate to their native language. (Be careful, though—going *too* slowly can be insulting.)

    *   Use simpler sentence structures, active-voice verbs ("speak" instead of "spoken to") and fewer stream-of-consciousness strings (several ideas linked together with commas). In other

---

[69]The Olympic Games are always a fascinating study in cultural differences, and having the Games in China in 2008 offered cultural experiences unlike anything else the American team had ever encountered. A well-documented example: gender attitudes.

Prior to the Games, my wife, Emily, joined me for a couple of weeks in China to sightsee prior to the craziness of the Games. One night, we were invited to a dinner with members of the Chinese Olympic Committee. The guest of honor was Mr. Joh, the senior member of their group. Mr. Joh was fascinated with Emily, and he asked many questions (through an interpreter) about her teaching career and her education. Ever articulate, Emily answered his questions completely and respectfully. After a while, he looked at me and asked, "Who is in charge in your home?" Emily and I looked at each other, smiled, and said, "No one, really." He smiled back, and spoke in English for the first time that evening. "Ahhh . . . democracy," he said. We all had a good laugh.

words, try to use shorter sentences and simple subject-verb-object construction.

- Avoid the colloquialisms that might make sense to an American but would be confusing to a non-American (for example, "We were just focused on *grinding through* the process, *one yard at a time*"). Remember that colloquialisms have two meanings: a literal one (he hit *a home run* in the baseball game) and a figurative one (our idea was well received; it was *a home run*). Figurative language requires extra translation—and time—on the part of a nonnative listener. Make the listener's job easier by avoiding this type of language altogether.

I'll close this section by directly addressing the concept of ethnocentricity. In many global organizations, the culture of the home office ends up dominating, and the people who sit in the home office often expect, consciously or subconsciously, the rest of the team around the world to adjust to their own cultural norms. The ivory tower syndrome can easily set in, and once it has set in, it is hard to undo. Leadership need to demonstrate through words and actions that they are interested in the opinions, needs, and contributions from everyone in the organization, not just those who sit in the home office every day.

**The Volunteer Team**

Here's the thing to remember about the Volunteer Team: The people on the team probably *want* to be there, but they are not *getting paid* to be there. If we rely too heavily on them, our expectations will not be met. This is because in most cases, those volunteers also have paying jobs that demand most of their attention.

Here are some things you can do to manage a team of volunteers successfully:

1. **Respect their time.** The key with the Volunteer Team is to find ways to keep great volunteers engaged without wearing them out. Don't schedule too many meetings, don't give them too many responsibilities, and don't make success or failure de-

pendent on any one single volunteer. You will eventually scare that volunteer away.

2. **Say thank you.** If you are not going to pay volunteers (and if you are going to expect them to spend their own money on travel and expenses without reimbursement), then, at a minimum, thank them generously and publicly. Some of your volunteers will want and need a little more public gratitude than others, but every volunteer appreciates at least a little. You will never go wrong saying thank you to a volunteer.

3. **Define roles.** Great volunteers are likely to be successful in the other areas of their lives. And successful people will be more willing to volunteer their time if they know what is expected of them. Successful people won't sign up and donate their time without knowing exactly what they are expected to contribute.

4. **Define boundaries.** It is critical with a Volunteer Team to also manage the person who has *too much* time on his or her hands and tries to get in there and run everything. In those cases, that volunteer may actually chase away other good volunteers, and often the volunteer who wants to run everything has another agenda in place: ego, insecurity, or perhaps a love of the spotlight. Be cautious of this volunteer, and don't let the effort become his or her own personal quest. You want volunteers who care about the cause and will support it selflessly.

5. **Balance the role of the volunteers and the role of the staff.** If you are part of an organization that has both volunteers and staff, this can get tricky. Where does the effort of the volunteer stop and that of the paid staff begin? What will the volunteers actually do, and how involved will they be in operations? How often will the staff be expected to consult with or inform the volunteers? When you have people working side by side, some paid, some not, the possibility exists for duplicated or wasted efforts, and lots of frustration. The only real solution here is to

ask lots of questions, have lots of dialogue, and write down ex-pected roles, norms, and behaviors for how the volunteers and staff will interact.

6. **Volunteers still need to be accountable.** Just because they are not getting paid does not mean they should not have ac-countability. "Free" labor has no value, or in fact, may have negative value, if that labor does not deliver as promised or expected. The organization needs to respect the volunteer, but the volunteer also needs to respect the organization and de-liver what he or she commits to.

In general, organizations that utilize both volunteers and staff tend to rely on the volunteers for fundraising, advice and counsel, relation-ships and introductions, and consulting on their area of expertise. Staff usually is expected to run operations and execute the plan. There are exceptions to every rule, of course. Occasionally volunteers may end up filling a gap in the staff, or they may have so much expertise and tal-ent that the organization needs them to do more. But the general rule still applies: clarify the roles of the volunteers and the staff.

**The Advisory Board**

The key to successfully managing the Advisory Board is to remem-ber its purpose: to advise.[70] Keeping people engaged when all you seek is their advice requires a few important things:

1. **Respect their time.** The types of people you will want advice from are successful. And successful people are usually very busy. Don't waste their time. Don't go to them constantly. Choose carefully when you do go to them and bring specific questions and information with you.

2. **Give them pitches they can hit.** Don't ask for advice that is well outside your advisors' areas of expertise. It will be easier

---

[70]The best example I know of is my own Advisory Board for The Latimer Group. Tom Lips, Phil Bonanno, Bryan Gild-enberg, Mike Davis, Josh Levine, and Bill Goggins all provide sage advice and counsel and the occasional important referral. I write to them and call them for advice regularly. We hold at least one annual conference call, and I write a thorough year-end report. I try to respect their time, and I always say thank you. It's a great group that has had a tangible impact on the growth of The Latimer Group.

to keep them engaged if they feel like they are making a difference. If you ask them for things that they cannot help you with, eventually they will question their involvement and lose interest. Consequently, you should build an Advisory Board from people well positioned to advise you. Think about the types of things you will need advice on, and then find good people who have the experience to help in those areas.

3.  **Take their advice.** You don't have to do everything the Advisory Board tells you to do, but you do have to follow their advice often enough to make them feel good about being involved. If you seldom take the advice of your board, they will eventually lose interest and drift away. In those times when you simply cannot take the board's advice, explain why you chose another route, and show gratitude for the advice and counsel given.

4.  **Report plans and results.** It is important to be able to communicate plans to your Advisory Board so they can see where you are taking the company or organization. Once they know the plan, their expertise may allow them to advise on things you didn't anticipate. Moreover, their value to you may increase and their enjoyment may grow. Besides sharing the plans, share the results. People want to be associated with success. (This is especially true for those successful people you want advising you.) Consider sharing written reports with your Advisory Board on a regular basis.

## The Team of Individual Producers

How do we create a team environment among people who don't really need each other in order to succeed? The best example is the national sales team, comprising people from all over the country who each sell in their own region. They don't need much from each other except perhaps the occasional knowledge share on what is working and what isn't. And even then, the members of this national sales team are also probably in a competitive dynamic where they each are trying to be the top salesperson. Perhaps there are even additional incentives for being at the top of the heap.[71]

So the question remains: How do we get people who don't need each other's support—and may actually compete with each other—to collaborate? It's not easy, but here are some strategies:

1. **Explain that we're better if we work together.** With our US Olympic Sailing Program, we preached the following to the athletes: If you all work separately and don't support each other, some of you will go to the Games and represent the United States and some of you will go home. If we work together, some of you will still go to the Games to represent the United States and some of you will still go home. But those who do go to the Games will stand a much greater chance of succeeding. This is because working together will make everyone a stronger competitor, and will give those who have qualified a much better shot at succeeding against the best. And if this happens, it will validate the efforts of everyone on the team—even those who did not win selection.

   Similarly, if everyone on a sales team works separately, only one member of the team will be the top performer in the company. But if everyone works together, each individual will enjoy better results, and whoever is the top performer at the company may even be a top performer within the entire industry. By working together, everyone will enjoy a higher level of production, and collectively the group will stand out among the entire industry.

---

[71]This is exactly the type of dynamic we have with our US Olympic and Paralympic Sailing Teams. In 2012, we have sent 22 sailors to represent the United States at the Olympic and Paralympic Games. These 22 sailors are spread across 13 events, some of them competing individually, some in teams of two, and some in teams of three. There are many little mini-teams within this larger team. And beyond these 22, there were perhaps as many as 50 others who were part of our national team leading up to Games selection, who were also competing for the right to represent the United States in 2012. How do you get all of these hyper-competitive people who all want the same thing to work together? Keep reading ...

2. **Create a strong team brand.** This point directly follows the first one but merits special mention. There is value in being associated with a winning team. If we all work together to make each other better, not only will we increase our own individual production levels, but we will also create a culture of success that will give us pride. The company might put more resources behind us, others will want to join our team, and the best leaders in the company will want to lead our team. There are lots of ways that a culture of winning will help the team, even though we all are graded based on our individual success. The leadership needs to point out how the success of the group benefits the individual.[72] Even though each competes alone, there is value for all if there is some group effort.

3. **Make some of the resources collective.** If all else fails, think about ways you can incentivize the individuals to begin acting like a team. Perhaps there are forms of support that you have provided individually, that could be shared collectively. Perhaps you could create financial incentives that reward the types of behavior you want to see more of. If you cannot persuade the group to begin acting like a team, think about ways you can push the new behaviors a bit more directly.

**Summary**

We all tend to throw the word "team" around quite liberally. But the concept of the team can take many forms, and each derivation of the concept needs to be thought about, and strategized for, a little differently. Having a reputation as a good teammate does not mean you

---

[72]In the Olympic sailing environment, this was easy. Every American Olympic aspirant needs to raise funds to compete. The US government does not provide direct support to its Olympic program, so the national teams (including the US Sailing Team) and the individual athletes have to find other ways to get funded. The athletes are very vocal about the resources they need from the national team, so the leadership of the national team is expected to raise money to create that support and infrastructure. We were able to, therefore, persuade the athletes that if we worked together, the collective results would be better. These results, we explained, would translate into more fundraising and, therefore, more support and structure from the national team. The results speak for themselves. In 2005, we were a $1 million-a-year program. Now, in 2012, we are a $4 million-a-year program. The athletes have seen the value of working together because it has directly translated into more support for them.

will fit perfectly on *every* kind of team; different types of teams require different behaviors.

One of the key concepts in this book has been that no two team situations are exactly the same. Different environments, different people, and different team scenarios present unique challenges.

Be aware of the changes and always be thinking about and asking yourself, "How will I need to act differently here if I am going to be successful?"

# SHARING THE SANDBOX

chapter 16: summary of key
concepts in part 2

*It's what you learn after you know it all that counts.*
**– John Wooden**

In Part 2 of *Sharing the Sandbox*, we moved beyond broad fundamentals and discussed specific steps you can take to build and lead your teams. Here are the key concepts from Part 2:

1. **Recognize alignment.** How do we know when our team is aligned? We know our team is aligned when all the energy on the team is focused outwardly at the competition or the issue at hand. If we are spending time and energy focused inwardly, debating incessantly, gossiping, and scheming, then we are certainly not aligned.

2. **Clarity on roles and responsibilities is essential.** The members of successful teams always know their own roles and understand the roles of everyone else on the team. Everyone knows their strengths and weaknesses and understands how all the pieces of the puzzle fit together. When we lack clarity on roles and responsibilities, we create the potential for gaps between team members' roles and things won't get done. We

also raise the likelihood of team frustration, as team members' roles may overlap too much.

3. **Respect is required and takes constant maintenance.** One person's respectful behavior is another person's rudeness. Great teams may not be filled with people who are best friends (they rarely are, in fact), but they are all based on internal respect for each other. Your opinion of what is respectful may be very disrespectful to me. This topic requires regular maintenance and communication to make sure we remain on the same page. And it is especially important to discuss after you bring someone new onto the team.

4. **Everyone needs to own the outcome.** We don't want people who just show up, punch the clock, do the absolute minimum, and then go home. We want people who will go above and beyond the specifics of their job description and who will care about the success of the team and the outcome of the project. We want people to treat the team's mission as if it were a prized possession of their own. Everyone treats a home they own more carefully and with more attention than one they rent. We want people to own their work—not rent it—and to approach it accordingly.

5. **Everyone has to substantively contribute to the bottom line.** Everyone does not have to contribute the exact same amount, and everyone does not have to contribute in the same way, but everyone has to do more than be a good presence—cheering for others and bringing a positive dynamic. Grossly disproportionate workloads or levels of responsibility will eventually lead to frustration and dysfunction.

6. **No two teams are the same.** I am always suspicious when I hear a leader say, "This is how I lead; it's always worked for me." That's not a long-term strategy for success. The best leaders in the 21st century will embrace that we have a more-informed, better-trained, and more-independent-minded workforce

than at any other point in human history. Therefore, if we are going to get this well-trained, well-informed, highly opinionated workforce to follow our lead, we need to read situations and adjust our approach based on the specifics of the moment. We still need to hold some fundamental principles as core to our approach, but beyond that, the way we apply those principles will change based on the situation and the people around us.

7. **Trust and credibility are the keys to the castle.** This topic could be a book unto itself, but at every step along the way, great leaders and teammates need to be thinking about how to build increasing levels of trust and credibility within their team. Without trust or credibility, you won't be able to lead anyone anywhere.

8. **Extreme personalities must be managed.** While I discourage labeling and blind judgments about the people around us, good leaders and managers also keep a keen eye out for certain extreme behavior patterns. This is because extreme personalities can derail your best efforts to build great teams. They need a little extra management, and if we are proactive and think ahead of time about how to handle tough situations, we'll allow less disruption when the challenging behaviors become obvious.

9. **What will you do if things fall apart?** Even the best teams, with the best leaders, can fall apart. How will you react if yours begins to show some cracks? Very often, a crumbling team situation can be saved before it becomes terminal. But your ability to save such a situation requires that you plan ahead of time and game out the "what if" scenarios.

# Part 2 Quizzes: Test Yourself

**Quiz #5: How aligned is your team?**

For each of the following questions, write the number corresponding to the answer that fits best.

1—High Confidence    2—Moderate Confidence
3—Low Confidence    4—No Confidence

1. Are you sure your team has clear goals and everyone knows what they are?    \_\_\_\_
2. Are you sure team members understand their roles and responsibilities?    \_\_\_\_
3. Are you sure team members are respectful towards each other?    \_\_\_\_
4. Are you sure each team member takes ownership over the outcome?    \_\_\_\_
5. Are you sure each team member carries his or her fair share of the workload?    \_\_\_\_
6. Are you sure the team is focused externally at the competition, and that they do not waste energy fighting each other?    \_\_\_\_
7. Are you sure the team is aligned and working together toward the common goal?    \_\_\_\_

**Total Score**    \_\_\_\_

**Rate your score:**

7-10: Highly Aligned
11-15: Moderately Aligned
16-20: Somewhat Aligned
21-28: Not at All Aligned

If you really want to test yourself, ask team members to take the same quiz and rate the team. Compare the answers. How did your own perception compare to the perceptions of others?

# PART 3

## Conclusions

THE LATIMER GROUP

# SHARING THE SANDBOX

chapter 17: hard questions with no easy answers

*The greatest challenge to any thinker is stating the problem in a way that will allow a solution.*

**– Bertrand Russell**

You've read it a few times already in *Sharing the Sandbox*, and I'll stand by it: Every team situation is different. Different people, challenges, and environments all combine to create different needs in every situation, and a formulaic approach to team building will, eventually, fail. The pursuit of business efficiency requires that we seek repeatable processes. Yet team-building style can seldom be duplicated with success. Building a team is an art, not a science. We simply cannot do things the same way every time.

Once we agree on this concept, we can then agree that the path to creating a strong team is hard to identify, the correct answers to team-building questions elusive. Each leader and teammate will view a team-building challenge in a different way and would almost certainly come up with a different approach.

I'll begin to wrap up *Sharing the Sandbox* by looking at some of the most challenging team-building questions I've dealt with. These have no easy answer, and depending on the day and the specifics of the situation, I might choose to answer these questions in different ways.

1.  **Does your team have to get along to succeed?** Throughout *Sharing the Sandbox*, we've been discussing topics like alignment and respect. One might make the assumption, therefore, that teams have to also get along to be successful. But is that really true? How far does the positive team dynamic have to extend? Do people have to *like* each other to be good teammates? I'm not sure.

    There are many examples of teams that succeeded despite deep personality conflicts.[73] And there are also plenty of examples of teams that got along famously but did not perform well. I've thought about this a great deal, and I just don't think there is a direct correlation between getting along and succeeding.

    But here is what I know for sure. To be good teammates, you don't need to vacation together, name your kids after each other, or even exchange Christmas cards. Being friendly outside of work is not required to be good teammates. What is required, at a minimum, is the commitment to treat your work relationship, and each other, with respect. We don't have to like each other personally to be good teammates. But we do have to respect each other professionally, and commit to work well together despite our personal differences.

    Looking back to chapter 10, where I introduced the concept of ARROW, friendship is not a prerequisite to alignment. Some will disagree with me on this. There are some smart people I know who believe that the better a team gets along, the more likely that team is to succeed. Such people believe that all the

---

[73] I'm a diehard baseball fan, and I have loved the New York Yankees for as long as I can remember. One of the best examples of teams that won despite real dislike among teammates was the 1978 Yankees championship team. There were fistfights in the locker room, guys who barely spoke to each other all season, and real dysfunction that has been catalogued in many books about that team, yet they still managed to win the 1978 World Series.

positive energy can have an impact on the outcome. Perhaps this is true, but I'm not convinced.

Let's take this a step further, and ask a related question. Can your team succeed if teammates actually *hate* each other? That's a harder one. I certainly believe that the greater the dislike among teammates, the more talented that team will need to be to succeed. Why? Because if there is legitimate dislike among teammates, ultimately they will find ways to spend energy focused inwardly on the fact that they do not like each other. As I mentioned earlier in this book, once you begin spending negative energy focused on your teammates, you are not focusing energy outwardly at the competition. And that is where the energy needs to be.

There are no easy answers to this question. But I'll stand by my belief that while teammates do not have to like each other personally, they have to respect each other professionally to be successful together.

2. **Is it OK to be good friends with a colleague?** The only acceptable answer to this question is that it depends. It depends on how complicated the work relationship is. It depends on how well you and your colleague can separate the personal and the professional. It depends on whether one of you is senior to the other, and whether the friendship will make that reporting relationship awkward.

My personal belief is that work becomes more tolerable and enjoyable when you can develop a rapport with a colleague and know enough about each other that you can converse about each other's lives a bit. In my experience, most of the time this works fine, and having some level of personal rapport and relationship enriches the work experience. However, when the personal friendship goes too far, or somehow gets in the way of the professional relationship, it can get messy pretty quickly. It's harder to critique, fire, make salary decisions about, demote, report on, or compete for advancement with someone with whom you have a friendship. Those sorts of work-related issues are much easier when the personal relationship is kept at arm's length.

This question can only truly be answered by you and you alone, and the answer will depend on your situation and preferences. There is no absolute truth here except this: Mix a personal relationship with a professional one only with great caution. Such a combination adds significant complexity. Tread carefully.

3.  **Should I always seek input from my team when making decisions?** We discussed this topic in chapter 8, but it merits another mention here, because it is not always easy.

    Collaboration is an important component to good team building. People like to be asked for their opinion, and in the 21st century, most people expect it. If we never collaborate, or if we never seek the input and opinion of others, we'll have a hard time keeping the team engaged and getting them to care about and own the success of the group. However, if we go too far in the other direction, seeking collaborative input all the time, we are likely to create an inefficient structure, where decisions get made slowly and every decision ends up as a compromise that satisfies no one completely.

    The correct answer here depends on the nature and urgency of the situation. The more time-critical or confidential the situation is, the more you should think about shrinking your decision-making loop. But I firmly believe that, under normal circumstances, the default setting for good team building should be a collaborative dynamic where people feel they can speak up. That said, in certain critical situations you should have the leadership confidence to seek a more efficient decision-making method.

    This topic is easy to understand in the abstract; the challenge for you will be to determine when to move away from that collaborative decision-making style and then when to come back to it. It depends on the situation and can only really be determined in the moment.

4. **Should the same rules apply to all team members, all the time?** This was also discussed in chapter 8, but again, it merits another mention. On one hand, consistency and rules within your team are good. You want everyone on the team to trust the system and trust that they have the same opportunities as others, but how far does that concept extend? Should everyone on the team be expected to act in exactly the same way, at exactly the same time as everyone else?

   Everyone on your team is different. Each of us is motivated in different ways. Each of us is most productive in a different environment. Each of us responds to different stimuli. So it might follow that everyone should be treated in a completely unique way. But I'm not suggesting that at all, because if everyone gets treated differently, with different rules, flexibilities, opportunities, and expectations, frustrations and a lack of trust will eventually arise.

   So the challenging question becomes this: What rules and expectations should apply to all, and where can the leader have some flexibility to do things differently for some? When we try to answer these questions, we realize yet again that team building is an art and not a science.

   Here's what I know: Some things need to be the same across the board for all members of the team, such as opportunities for advancement and benefits, and a positive, respectful work environment. Also, everyone should be required to substantively contribute to the bottom line. Your list may look different from mine, but we can all agree that there are some things that should apply to all. But where does that end and when can the leader start to have some latitude to do things a little differently?

Once again, it depends. How new is the leader in his or her role? How much trust is there? How well aligned is the team? What are the expectations and behavioral norms within the company or the industry?

In my experience, I have been happy to let people have some flexibility in how they operate, such as when they come in to work, when they leave, and how often they work from home. But in the areas where I allow for flexibility, I make some expectations clear: If you are working from home, when will you be online and available? If you need to cut off work at 3 p.m. to pick up your child from school, when will you be back online and available later in the day? If I am going to trust and respect you by giving you some flexibility, then you have to earn that trust and respect me and the group by working as hard as (if not harder than) you would normally.

Again, this is art, not science. I believe in trusting people who work with me, and if I am in the leadership position, I believe in giving lots of leeway and opportunity for differentiation. But in return, I require respect for me and for the rest of the team. The latitude can't be met with disrespect or be taken advantage of. (For some people, "working from home" is code for starting later, ending earlier, and a really inefficient and unproductive workday.) If different rules are going to apply to different people, then the trust and respect has to flow in both directions.

My answer to this question is this: Everyone on your team has to be treated exactly the same way on certain things (salary and advancement opportunities, expectations for productivity, and so forth), but you can have some flexibility on *how* people get their work done. The amount of room you give people depends on you, your team, and the situation. There is no one single way to answer this question.

# SHARING THE SANDBOX

*I've finally arrived at the age at which the things I remember*
*most clearly never happened at all.*
*– Mark Twain*

Can something be both simple and complex? I think so. The concepts of team building, and everything discussed in this book, are not complicated. The ideas are simple enough, and I highly doubt that I've presented anything earth shattering or groundbreaking here. But the execution of the simple concepts, and the discipline required to lead well on a consistent basis, is more complicated.

Why? Because of a little thing called "the ego" that tends to get in the way when we are leading other people. The ego will try to convince us that we are better than we really are, that leadership means people should be serving us, and that different rules apply to us. But none of those things is true. While a little ego can be healthy, having too much will cause us problems.

If you flip back through this book and think about the common denominators of the many ideas contained in it, I think a few things will stand out:

1. **Great team building and team leadership are not about you.** Success requires a focus on and an understanding of the people around you and what you will have to do to serve them well. This idea is central to everything we've discussed within these pages. When you lead the team, you are (or should be) in service to others, not the other way around. Great team leadership requires that we figure out what will make our team members successful, and then use our influence as the leader to clear roadblocks to performance.

2. **One size does *not* fit all.** People are different. Teams are different. Situations are different. While it is always advisable to have certain principles that matter most to you, it is inadvisable to become so attached to *your* style or *your* methods that you attempt to apply the same strategy, tactics, or plan over and over and over again. If you find yourself saying things like "It's always worked for me in the past, so I'll keep doing it," please look around for the guy waving a figurative red flag. That will be me, trying to warn you that you have gotten too set in your ways. Just because something has worked before does not mean it will work again. To remain relevant as a team leader, you'll have to evaluate your past leadership successes and make objective judgments on what's needed in the current situation. The world is constantly changing, and team leaders need to change along with it.

3. **Goals are required for success.** This topic has come up throughout the book in a variety of different ways. Goals give us something to work toward. They inform every decision we make. When we have clear goals, it's like having a map with a specific destination we are trying to reach. When we don't have clear goals, it's like we're taking an aimless walk in the woods, hoping we get somewhere good, but without any way to evaluate when we have arrived. There are many things that matter when it comes to team building, but without clarity on goals, nothing else matters.

4. **Leadership brings scrutiny.** You want to lead? Then you'd better be ready to be held to a higher standard than everyone else, where every word you speak and every action you take are examined closely and evaluated by your peers. Prepare to lead by example.

5. **We all need to learn how to follow before we can learn how to lead.** No one leads all the time, and being a good leader starts with knowing how to be a good teammate. When we learn how to follow others, we've begun to internalize that we are not the star of the show all the time. This is one of the most important lessons in learning how to lead. Good followership is about being a good, supportive teammate. And so is good leadership.

6. **Good communication skills are required for success.** Think about all the things we've discussed in this book, and you'll see that communication skills are a common thread. Team building, leadership, and followership are all about understanding the people around you, asking questions, listening to answers, sharing decisions (and the logic behind them), discussing plans, etc. The list goes on, but everything on this list is a form of communication. Teams are not solitary ventures. They are collaborative ones, and collaboration requires communication.

7. **ARROW is your friend.** Great leadership and great teams are about, above all else, alignment, but alignment is at times elusive. So, when we can find a way to identify and pursue the key elements, we have a competitive advantage. All of the elements of ARROW (roles and responsibilities, respect, ownership, and a willingness to work) are important on their own, but when we can bring all the elements together, we have the opportunity to create something truly special.

**Final Thoughts**

I'll close this book exactly where I started, and repeat some of the initial thoughts from the introduction. The business world's reliance on teams is constant. Our business culture is dominated by all kinds of them: project teams, cross-functional teams, virtual teams, global teams, boards. Teams are everywhere. We are expected to contribute toward the good of them; if we seek advancement, we are expected to be able to lead them; and we are constantly judged by our ability to boost their productivity.

It is my sincere hope that this book helps you become a stronger partner, teammate, leader, and manager of people. If we can harness the skills to become better teammates, if we can learn how to consistently build strong teams, if we can learn to take joy not just from our own success but from the success of others and of the group, if we can learn to motivate people and cause them to *want* to work together, if we can learn to create an environment where human beings can thrive and succeed together, if we can learn to play well with others and share the sandbox with respect, we will have perhaps the most-sought-after skill in the 21st century. We will have significant competitive advantage and create enormous value for ourselves and everyone around us.

Good luck!

# INDEX